healing
reiki

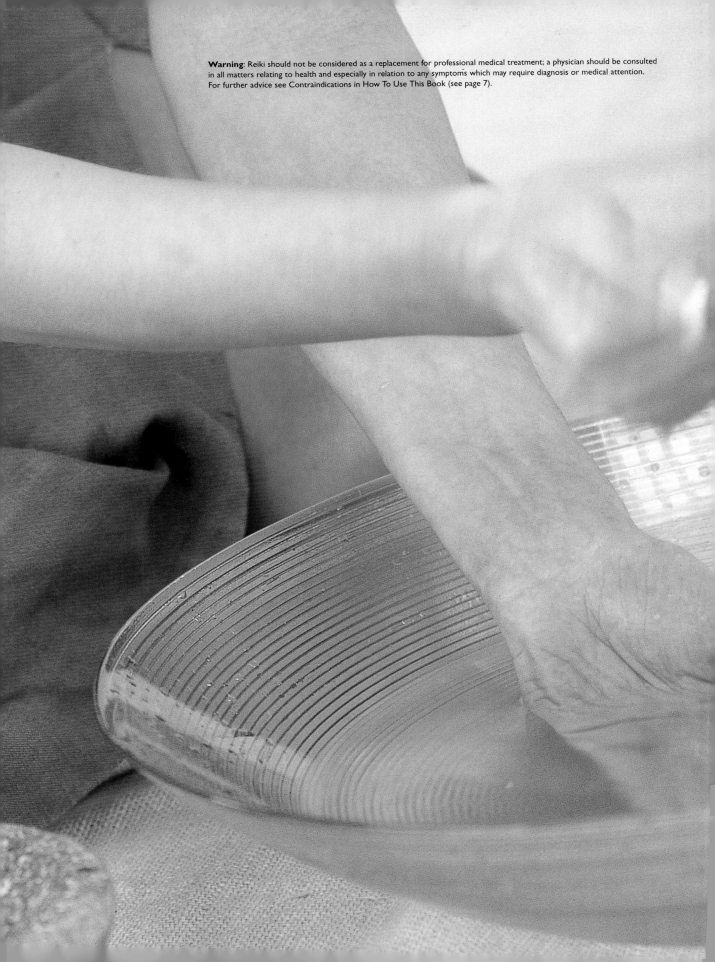

healing reiki

Eleanor McKenzie

HAMLYN

contents

how to use this book

To become a Reiki practitioner requires the receiving of attunements from a Reiki Master. This book is not a substitute for attending a Reiki class but is intended rather as an introduction for those who wish to learn more about Reiki and as a work of reference to guide the initiated.

The book is divided into five main sections with an additional Foreword and introductory sections written by Reiki Master Don Alexander. The Introduction explains what Reiki is and examines the concept of energy. The Eastern system of *chakras* is discussed with reference to the human anatomy and the endocrine system. Other forms of energy healing are also examined, including Traditional Chinese Medicine, Qigong, Acupuncture, Reflexology and Bach Flower Remedies. The Introduction includes tips on how to prepare for Reiki and on ways to use Reiki on plants and flowers, food and drink, and animals. It also includes important medical questions about what kind of case history you will need to obtain from your patient prior to commencing treatment.

The second section explores the Historical and Spiritual Principles of Reiki. The story of the three Masters is explained in detail along with a discussion of the differences and diversions which are involved in the current Reiki debate. The Five Spiritual Principles are included, as is a discussion of what to expect from the three levels of Reiki initiation. The problems of choosing a Reiki Master are covered, including the current differences of approach to teaching Reiki. The various

meanings of well-known symbols are also discussed in relation to the use of symbols in Reiki. The Reiki symbols referred to in this book should be learnt from a Reiki Master during Second and Third Degree Initiations.

Self-Treatment provides a step-by-step guide to giving yourself full body treatments. This section emphasizes the importance of achieving a balance within the self before attempting to practise Reiki on others. This section features the main positions for self-treatment taught by the traditional Usui school along with a number of optional variations.

Similarly, Treating Others provides clear guidance on how to give a full body treatment. With easy-to-follow instructions, accompanied by step-by-step photography, this section includes the main positions which would traditionally be included in a one hour treatment. This section also includes instructions on how to give group treatments and how to treat babies and children who can benefit greatly from Reiki.

The final section covers the use of Reiki for Remedial Treatment. It is important to note here that Reiki should never be used as a substitute for orthodox medical treatment. Opening with a section on the use of Reiki in acute and chronic conditions, there is an

exploration of the variable patterns of healing. This section also includes a short directory of first aid for common ailments and accidents. Within this section you will find information and advice on orthodox medical treatment, Reiki treatment and other complementary therapies for the following problems: acute toothache, broken bones, burns and scalds, cuts and abrasions, headaches and migraines, and shock. Any complementary treatments covered in this directory are included in the glossary which can be found at the back of the book.

The book concludes with a short series of real-life case studies which highlight the potential for Reiki to heal, soothe and strengthen those who practise and receive it.

Contraindications	Treatment tips

All techniques included in this book are intended as a guide and should not be used as a substitute for orthodox medical treatment.

- I would recommend extreme caution if you are asked to treat someone with a pacemaker. The effect of Reiki energy on such a device can be very unpredictable.

- Do not give Reiki to broken bones before the site of the break has been set in plaster. Otherwise there is a real chance that the bone may start to knit at an incorrect angle.

- Extreme care should be taken when treating anyone who suffers from diabetes. Reiki can affect the levels of insulin required by the body. You will need to warn the recipient that if they wish to receive Reiki, they will need to monitor their insulin levels very closely.

- Care should be taken during all stages of pregnancy with the use of essential oils and pressure points.

- It is important to remember that whilst it is safe to give Reiki to babies and children, they do not need to receive Reiki for as long as an adult. Twenty to thirty minutes should be adequate for a full body treatment.

- Do not attempt to give or receive Reiki after drinking alcohol as it may cause some unpleasant side effects.

- Make sure that the environment in which you give Reiki treatments is warm, well aired and relaxing.

- Ideally, use a massage table to give Reiki treatments but you could use a firm bed or a duvet placed on the floor.

- Remove any jewellery you are wearing such as rings, bracelets and watch.

- Always wash your hands immediately before and after each treatment.

- Grounding exercises (see page 35) can be useful as a preparation for giving a Reiki treatment.

- You could rub a few drops of rose oil or other oil of your choice on your hands before giving a treatment.

- Try playing soothing music quietly in the background to help create a relaxing environment.

- Sit quietly for a few minutes before your client arrives to clear your mind. You could even give yourself Reiki to the heart and solar plexus areas.

foreword

'Since the word got about that "everybody can be a healer", the teaching and practice of Reiki has spread all over the world. This phenomenal expansion has brought with it renewed interest and research into its origins – its historical, cultural, philosophical and spiritual roots. We should remind ourselves, however, that Reiki exists only through its practice. Without the "laying on of hands", or the touching of hearts in distance healing through the evocation of the Reiki symbols, there is no Reiki.

It is a relief to realize that profound healing can occur without either the healer or, for that matter, the sick person needing to know anything of the causes or the nature of the illness. As a healing art, Reiki does not threaten the authority of orthodox medicine. It is not another cure for colds, carbuncles, cancer or, for that matter, anything else. The practitioner of Reiki makes no such claims. Reiki, being entirely holistic, helps the sick person heal from within, irrespective of the symptoms. It is eminently practical and simple and therein lies its attraction.

In Anglo-Saxon times there was a word *hál*. It meant "whole", it meant "healthy", and it meant "holy". *Hál*, although now virtually obsolete, survives in certain modern words and phrases such as "halo", "hallowed" and "hale and hearty". However, our modern language does not now include a linguistic equivalent to *hál* and we are left with three distinct and often apparently unrelated words.

Reiki is personal and holistic – it unites the concepts of *hál*. It helps people become whole. As people become whole, so they become well. More often than not the healing can be seen and felt in the body, and the symptoms ease or disappear. Sometimes the body does not get well, yet even so a profound healing occurs. A lifetime becomes complete.

Perhaps there is only one healer, love. At those times when I am less loving I experience myself as being apart from you, from others and from the events of the world. When, on the other hand, I am more loving, I feel less fragmented and closer to you and to others. I feel whole. All my experience tells me that love heals by making whole and that Reiki itself is an expression of love.

What is remarkable about Reiki is that it can be passed on so simply to anyone who wants it. The Reiki passed down from Master to student today is as pristine, as pure as when the Grand Master, Dr Usui, transmitted it to his first students in Japan over 100 years ago.

Attempts to define Reiki often fail. Reiki is a mode of personal being. When you are in Reiki mode, a touch, a simple process of caringly placed hands can work wonders. When you are in Reiki mode, the same hands that dig the garden, wash the dishes or take the wheel of a car become hands of energy and light.

If you are already experienced in the practice of Reiki you will understand what I mean. If you are just about to embark on your Reiki adventure for the first time then you will soon know from your own experience what this book describes so well.

One of the best ways of learning more about Reiki at first hand is to visit an open evening. Here you can experience Reiki for yourself and meet people who practise Reiki both privately and professionally. It is a good way to make instant friends when travelling abroad. Reiki Associations in your home country will often be able to put you in contact with associations in the country you plan to visit.'

Reiki Master **Don Alexander**

introduction

There are as many paths to enlightenment as there are people. Reiki is one of those paths and each person who practises it will walk the path in their own way. No one person owns it – it has been given to all of us as part of the essence of our human being.

Reiki is primarily perceived as a practice for healing the body, but it is also a method for healing the mind and spirit. Ultimately, Reiki has the power to reunite the trinity of Mind-Body-Spirit in their optimal state of harmony. All of us need to start the process of returning to that state of harmony. Reiki, with its power and simplicity and its methods for healing both the self and others, offers the way to start taking what I call 'the journey home'.

what is reiki?

Reiki (pronounced ray-key) is a Japanese word meaning 'universal life energy'. In Japanese it is represented by two *kanji* or pictograms; the first, Rei, may be translated as 'universal, transcendental spirit, a boundless essence'. The second, *Ki*, translates as 'life force energy'. This life force energy can be defined as that energy which resides and acts in all created matter – animal, vegetable or mineral. In *Awaken Healing Light of the Tao*, Mantak Chia, an authority on Qigong, an ancient Chinese discipline for utilizing *Chi* (the Chinese equivalent of *Ki*) in the body, defines *Chi/Ki* as energy, air, breath, wind, vital breath, vital essence – the activating energy of the universe. When this force leaves the body then life has departed.

In all cultures and religions there is a name or concept which corresponds to the meaning of *Ki* in Reiki, although some of the theories concerning them may be quite different. The best-known of these are:

Chi – found in Chinese medicine, for example acupuncture and Qigong
Prana – found in the Hindu *Upanishads* and yoga
Light – found in Christian teachings

Everything that is alive contains *Ki* and radiates it, but the person who has received the Reiki attunements or initiation (see pages 54 and 56) has their body's energy channels opened in a way that connects them to the Universe's limitless source of *Ki*. The person now has unlimited access to the life force energy for their own healing and is also a channel for transmitting this energy to others.

Reiki is healing energy in its truest sense. When the Reiki practitioner channels this life energy through their hands to the recipient, it activates the body's natural ability to heal itself. The energy goes to the deepest levels of a person's being, where illnesses have their origin. It works wherever the recipient needs it most, releasing blocked energies, cleansing the body of toxins and working to create a state of balance. It reinforces the recipient's ability to take responsibility for their life, and helps them to make the necessary changes in attitude and lifestyle to promote a happier and healthier life.

What sets Reiki apart from other healing methods is the process of attunement. Reiki may appear to be similar to the laying on of hands and other types of touch healing, but the process of opening up the energy channels via the attunements is quite distinctive. Reiki is also different to other healing methods because the attunement is not giving the person something new; instead it is simply unlocking what was always there. It is just like switching on a light – the electricity is present, but someone has to press the switch to activate it.

Reiki is also differentiated from other healing systems by its simplicity. Following the initial attunements you only have to place your hands on yourself or another person and Reiki will be drawn from the universe (not from you), flowing through your hands to whatever part of the body you are touching. There are no complicated mental exercises and no fasting or prolonged meditation practice required in order to practise Reiki. Once initiated, the ability to channel this life energy is always with you.

Reiki is a healing system that is a safe, natural and holistic way of treating many acute and chronic conditions and bringing about spiritual, mental and emotional wellbeing. These conditions include stress, sinusitis, menstrual problems, cystitis, migraine, asthma, M.E. (chronic fatigue syndrome), eczema, arthritis, menopausal problems, back pain, anxiety, tension, depression, insomnia and sciatica. Reiki is suitable for everyone, including the very young and the elderly, pregnant women and those recovering from surgery. It is also a great tonic, and if you are in good health Reiki will help you to stay that way.

As is the case with all alternative healing, Reiki should not be used as a substitute for orthodox medicine, although individuals may choose to do so, and that is their right. No Reiki practitioner, however, should advise any person receiving the therapy to stop taking prescribed medicines or not to see a doctor.

Reiki is also much more than a method of healing the physical body. Once it has been integrated into our daily lives it opens the heart to experience a unity with the divine and to reconnect us with the eternal oneness of all creation. There are many experiences to be had through practising Reiki, but perhaps none is more beautiful than the recognition of the universal spirit that unites us all. For so long many of us have denied the spirit within us, making ourselves ever more fragile in the process. Through practising Reiki we can once more strengthen ourselves spiritually and begin to experience fully all aspects of our humanity and the Earth as we were meant to.

To become a Reiki practitioner requires the receiving of attunements from a Reiki Master who has also received the attunements and training. Reiki cannot be learned from a book, but, as with many healing practices, books can act as our supports and guides after we have learnt a subject, or they can introduce us to a subject that we feel we would like to know more about. This book is not a substitute for attending a Reiki class; it is a reference tool for those who are already initiated and an introduction to Reiki for those who wish to experience its healing powers.

the endocrine system and the *chakras*

in the etheric body, is understood to be interconnected, with the endocrine system acting as a conveyor of energy to the *chakras* and vice versa. The precise way in which this exchange of energy works cannot be clinically demonstrated, which is why medical science is sceptical of it, although the relationship between energy and matter is now well established in science. Those who work with Reiki, or who work with the *chakras* through other methods, know it intuitively to be real. But to appreciate more fully

It is the aim of every Reiki treatment to channel Reiki to all parts of the body. In this way the energy works to bring balance and healing to the whole person. One unique aspect of Reiki is that the energy has an intelligence of its own and that attempts by the giver to direct the energy do not work. For example, if you have back pain and receive a Reiki treatment, the practitioner will treat your whole body and will give extra attention to your painful back. But the practitioner cannot direct the energy to go only into healing the back pain, so there is no guarantee that you will leave with your back cured. The energy will go first to where it is needed most in your body, and that may not be your back, even though it is the place where symptoms are apparent. This is why several treatments, each lasting 1–1½ hours, are usually needed and why the Reiki practitioner should not try to direct the energy during a treatment, but instead remain an open channel.

The practice as taught by Mrs Takata, on which most practice in the West is based with some variation of hand positions, ensures a full body treatment which includes the whole endocrine system and with it the *chakras*. In Reiki, and in other healing methods, the relationship between these two systems, one based in the physical body and one

the endocrine system

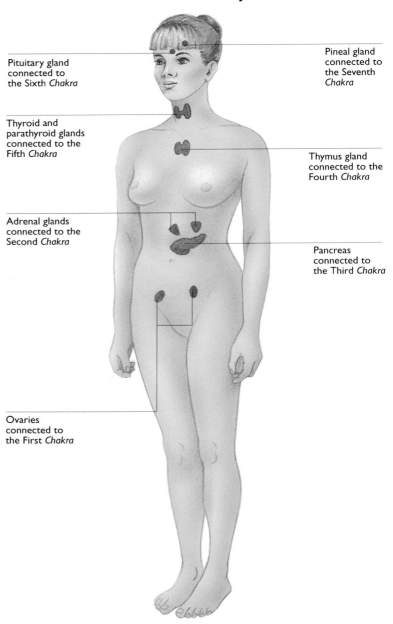

Pituitary gland connected to the Sixth *Chakra*

Pineal gland connected to the Seventh *Chakra*

Thyroid and parathyroid glands connected to the Fifth *Chakra*

Thymus gland connected to the Fourth *Chakra*

Adrenal glands connected to the Second *Chakra*

Pancreas connected to the Third *Chakra*

Ovaries connected to the First *Chakra*

the relationship between the two systems it is necessary to have an understanding of the way in which both of them work.

The endocrine system
The glands of the system are:

The pituitary
The pineal
The thyroid and parathyroids
The thymus
The islets of Langerhans in the
    pancreas
The adrenals
The gonads in men and the ovaries
    in women

The function of the endocrine system is to secrete chemicals called hormones throughout the body via the bloodstream, and in doing so to regulate the action of the organs and tissues. Hormones also react to stress, help the body fight infection and are essential for reproduction. Malfunction of the endocrine system leads to problems strongly suggestive of the concept of imbalance: diabetes, hypothyroidism, hyperthyroidism and infertility, all of which are caused by hormone levels being either too high or too low. Hormones, once out of balance, are not easily rebalanced, as anyone with a thyroid problem will testify, demonstrating that the range within which they must fall for optimum health is quite precise. I doubt that many of us, even if we are not manifesting illnesses of the endocrine system, have optimum hormone levels because we have so much stress in our lives – and we also have no time to relieve it.

The main gland of the endocrine system is the pituitary, which resides in the brain along with the pineal gland. The pituitary coordinates all the other glands and also produces the hormones that influence growth, urine production and uterine contractions.

The thyroid gland, which is in the neck, controls metabolism. When it is not secreting enough of the hormone thyroxine, the imbalance called hypothyroidism occurs. This is characterized by sluggishness, weight gain, coldness and depression. When the gland is secreting too much thyroxine, hyperthyroidism occurs. This is characterized by weight loss, sweating and heart palpitations. The parathyroids, located on each lobe of the main gland, are essential for the maintenance of healthy bones, nerves and muscles, and they also balance calcium and phosphorus levels in the body.

The thymus, located in the chest cavity near to the heart, is essential to the maintenance of a healthy immune system.

the human anatomy

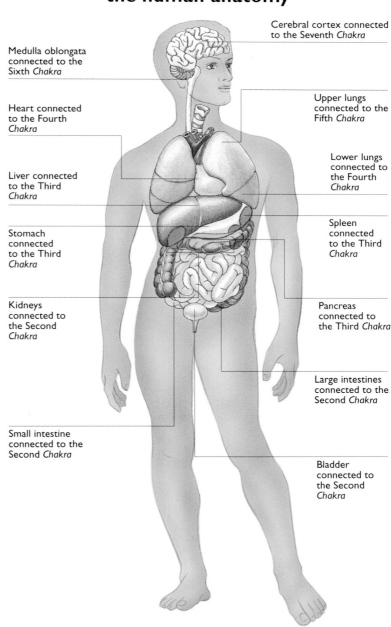

Medulla oblongata connected to the Sixth *Chakra*

Heart connected to the Fourth *Chakra*

Liver connected to the Third *Chakra*

Stomach connected to the Third *Chakra*

Kidneys connected to the Second *Chakra*

Small intestine connected to the Second *Chakra*

Cerebral cortex connected to the Seventh *Chakra*

Upper lungs connected to the Fifth *Chakra*

Lower lungs connected to the Fourth *Chakra*

Spleen connected to the Third *Chakra*

Pancreas connected to the Third *Chakra*

Large intestines connected to the Second *Chakra*

Bladder connected to the Second *Chakra*

The islets of Langerhans are in the pancreas and are responsible for the secretion of insulin and glucogen to maintain correct levels of glucose in the blood. When insufficient insulin is produced, glucose levels in the blood rise, resulting in diabetes mellitus.

The adrenal glands lie above the kidneys. They produce two main types of hormone: the outer layer produces steroid hormones that balance the salt, sugar and water concentration in the body, while the inner layer produces the adrenalin necessary to stimulate the 'fight or flight' reaction.

The gonads and ovaries secrete hormones necessary for reproduction. Women suffering from an imbalance of hormone secretion in the ovaries manifest symptoms varying from infertility to irregular menstruation and PMS.

The *chakra* system

Chakra is a Sanskrit word meaning 'wheel'. There are seven *chakras* in the etheric body, with the first situated at the base of the spine and the seventh on the crown of the head. They are traditionally visually depicted as a lotus flower, which, when combined with the symbolism of the wheel, results in a circular shape spinning around its centre as individual petals unfold. Each *chakra* has a number of attributes, including a colour, a relation to an element and the maintenance of specific physical and emotional functions (see the table below).

It is spiritually significant that the colours of the *chakra* system make a rainbow. In a number of cultures the rainbow represents a bridge between this world and that of the gods, and in Christian culture it signifies God's forgiveness and His covenant with mankind. Also, the number seven is the sum of the number of divinity (three) and the number of mankind (four) and represents the macrocosm and the microcosm or the relationship between the divine and humanity.

The way in which the *chakras* influence the health of the physical body may be described in terms of the Hermetic paradigm, 'As above, so below.' The invisible etheric body where the *chakras* are located vibrates at a higher frequency than the dense lower-frequency physical body. Imbalances in the higher frequency flow down to the physical, thus creating disease. Imbalance can be seen in the *chakra* as either a slowing of the speed at which it spins and a diminution of its size, corresponding to underworking in the physical organs, or, conversely, the *chakras* can spin too fast and open too wide, also leading to physical and emotional problems. This is often experienced in the solar plexus *chakra* when the adrenals are overworked as a result of stress.

Although most of us cannot see the *chakras*, it is possible to become familiar with how they are working by focusing attention on their locations and concentrating on how the area feels. Ironically, it is probably easier to 'read' your *chakras* when you are experiencing an extreme of emotion or physical difficulty. It is also possible to

Right: There are seven *chakras* in the etheric body. In the East, the *chakras* are often depicted as lotus flowers, each petal symbolizing the blossoming of a particular quality or attribute. Each *chakra* is associated with different spiritual and physical functions.

	NAME	LOCATION	COLOUR	ELEMENT	FUNCTION	ENDOCRINE GLAND
First *Chakra*	Muladhara	Base of spine/ perineum	Red	Earth	Survival and prosperity	Gonads/ovaries
Second *Chakra*	Swadisthana	2.5–7.5 cm/1–3 inches below the navel	Orange	Water	Physical and sexual health	Lymphatic glands/ adrenals
Third *Chakra*	Manipura	Solar plexus	Yellow	Fire	Personal power/ emotions	Pancreas/adrenals
Fourth *Chakra*	Anahata	By the heart in the centre of the chest	Green/Rose	Air	Love	Thymus
Fifth *Chakra*	Vishudda	Middle of the throat	Blue	Ether	Communication	Thyroid
Sixth *Chakra*	Ajna	Between and slightly above the eyebrows	Indigo	None	Intuition	Pineal
Seventh *Chakra*	Sahasrara	Crown of the head	Violet/White	None	Spirituality	Pituitary

influence the state of your *chakras* by the colours you wear or by meditating on specific colours and even by the colour of the food you eat.

The *chakra* system is complex and requires much study in order to appreciate its subtleties fully. Giving Reiki treatments to oneself and to others on a regular basis will greatly help you to intuit where there are imbalances in the *chakras* and full body treatments will ensure that you treat any imbalances in both the endocrine system and the *chakra* system.

Case study

A friend asked me to give him a Reiki treatment as he had heard a lot about it but had never experienced it. He always appeared outgoing and confident and had a very pleasant speaking voice. After I had finished the treatment I told him that I had felt an imbalance in the throat area and suggested that he wore something blue or silver near to the throat *chakra*. He then told me that he had started a postgraduate course and felt nervous about speaking in front of other students. I thought this was surprising, given his outward demeanour, but it confirmed what I had felt while giving him Reiki. Some weeks later he told me that he had found a blue stone and worn it around it his neck, and afterwards he was able to speak in class without any problem.

other forms of healing

The *Ki* in Reiki, the universal life energy, corresponds to *Chi* in the Chinese systems of Qigong and acupuncture and to the concept of *prana* in the various Indian systems of yoga. In order to appreciate the uniqueness and simplicity of Reiki, it is useful to understand the ways in which other therapies approach the manipulation or balancing of this energy. Additionally, an understanding of other healing methods will help in the treatment of oneself and others, even though Reiki is felt by many to be sufficient in itself. Moreover, I think that if you are giving a treatment and intuit that the receiver would benefit from a bodywork or other therapy, it is better to make such a recommendation from a position of some knowledge. This can be gained by reading up on the subject and also by exchanging treatments with other non-Reiki therapists, thus enabling you to gain experience that you can share with others. If you do recommend other therapies to the person you are treating, you should make it clear that it is just a suggestion and that they should only pursue it if it feels right for them.

Below is a discussion of other healing methods, including Qigong, acupuncture, reflexology and Bach flower remedies. These are all very different, but, like Reiki, they are all based on the concept of the intangible (energy) affecting the tangible (physical matter) and in some instances vice versa. The explanations are not in-depth – they are simply meant as preliminary guides to systems that can complement and enhance your Reiki practice. References to specialist books on these subjects can be found in the bibliography at the end of this book.

Traditional Chinese Medicine

Both Qigong and acupuncture come from Traditional Chinese Medicine (TCM). They are based on the same underlying system, that of the meridians.

The meridians

The meridians, which are a primary feature of the Oriental energy anatomy, are lines or channels in the body that conduct *Chi* or energy. They are considered to be separate from all the other anatomical systems, for example the nervous system or the lymphatic system, although they run parallel to the physical systems and are complementary to them. The meridians are considered to be a 'control system', operating at a higher level than the physical but directly affecting it. There is an obvious similarity between this concept and that of the *chakras*, even if the structures are dissimilar.

There are a total of 35 meridians in the system, conducting *Chi* throughout the body. These include 12 major meridians, 8 extra meridians and 15 collateral channels. It is along the 12 major meridians and 2 of the extra meridians (known as the Governor and Conception channels) that the 'acupoints' are found. These are used to effect changes in the energy system.

The major meridians

The major meridians are each related and connected to a specific organ. In the West, each one is called by the name of the relevant organ, such as the heart, lungs, kidneys and so on (see page 25). However, each meridian does not relate solely to its corresponding organ but also to many other aspects of the person, both physical and emotional. For example, just as each *chakra* has a corresponding element (see page 22), so do the meridians. The meridians connected to the element of Earth are the stomach and the spleen. These are then connected to the colour yellow (as is the Third *Chakra*), to sympathy (emotion), sweet (taste), flesh (tissue) and damp (climate). A full explanation of these and what is known as a Table of Correspondences can be found in most good books on Traditional Chinese Medicine.

The Governor and Conception channels

These two channels and the 12 major meridians are the only places where acupoints are located. The Governor channel, which runs up the centre of the back and over the top of the head, ending on the upper lip, has 28 points. The Conception channel, which runs up the centre front and ends at the bottom lip, has 24 points. As part of the Eight Meridians, these channels are considered to be reservoirs of energy that can be drawn on when there is a deficiency. Some of the central exercises of Qigong involve circulating *Chi* through the Governor and Conception channels, also known as the Microcosmic Orbit.

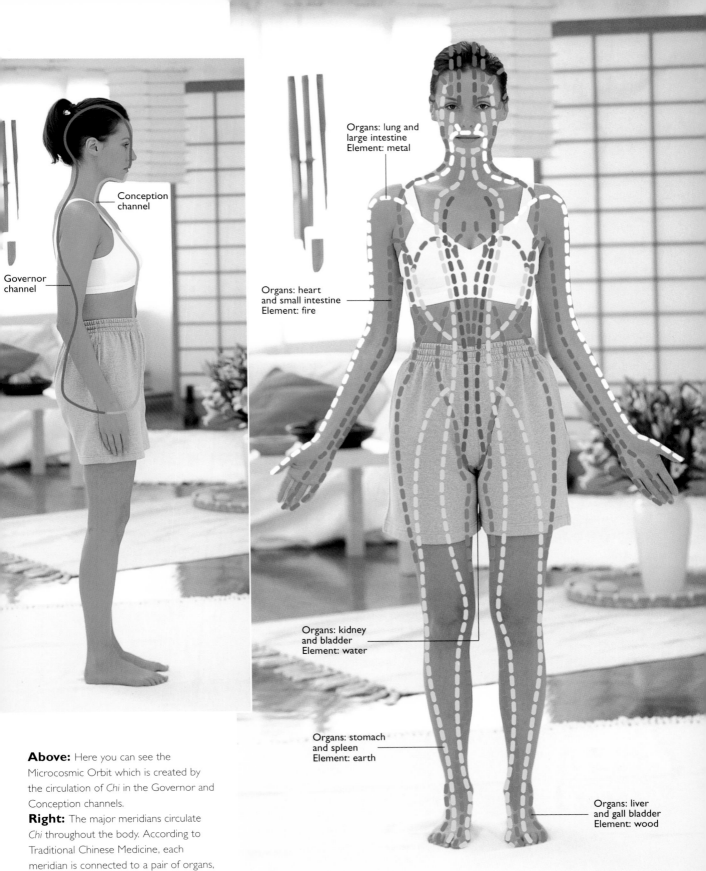

Conception
channel

Governor
channel

Organs: lung and
large intestine
Element: metal

Organs: heart
and small intestine
Element: fire

Organs: kidney
and bladder
Element: water

Organs: stomach
and spleen
Element: earth

Organs: liver
and gall bladder
Element: wood

Above: Here you can see the
Microcosmic Orbit which is created by
the circulation of *Chi* in the Governor and
Conception channels.
Right: The major meridians circulate
Chi throughout the body. According to
Traditional Chinese Medicine, each
meridian is connected to a pair of organs,
a colour and an element.

Qigong

In *Chi Kung*, James MacRitchie quotes from *The Spring and Autumn Annals*, a Chinese history book written in 230 BC by Master Lu, who refers to the fact that 'a long, long time ago dancing was used to aid the flow of *Chi* and blood'. A more detailed and systematic description of the origins, theory and practice of Qigong is to be found in the classic medical text of the same period, *The Yellow Emperor's Classic of Internal Medicine*. These references establish the antiquity of Qigong, although, ironically, it is only in the last 20 years that it has enjoyed a resurgence in China, where some 60 million people are said to be currently practising it.

Qigong is a broad term for a practice with many different styles. The word itself means 'energy cultivation'. Based on utilizing the meridian system, the aim of Qigong is to prevent disease and promote longevity through daily practice. By using gentle stretching exercises combined with breathing techniques and visualization it balances the flow of energy through the meridians, thereby affecting the state of the physical organs. Where there is a stagnation of energy, Qigong exercises provide an unblocking mechanism, acting in much the same way that channelling Reiki also unblocks energy. Although Qigong primarily works with energy already in the system, its breathing techniques draw *Chi* into the body. This is comparable to the drawing in of Reiki energy by the receiver through the hands of the giver.

Acupuncture

Acupuncture is probably one of the best-established complementary methods of healing in the West and is now offered by many doctors in hospitals and GP clinics. Unlike most other complementary methods, acupuncture has been the subject of clinical trials that have proved its effectiveness in treating many diseases and their symptoms, the most notable being pain.

Acupuncture is perhaps more ancient than Qigong, and stone acupuncture needles dating from the Neolithic period have been found in Mongolia. But, like Qigong, the earliest detailed commentary on acupuncture is in *The Yellow Emperor's Classic of Internal Medicine*. For the Chinese, acupuncture is used as a means of prevention of disease as well as a cure, although it is primarily used in the West as a cure.

Acupuncture uses the technique of inserting very fine needles into the skin at the acupoints on the meridians. The needles act to stimulate these points and, in so doing, balance the flow of energy in the body. Acupressure uses the same points but employs the fingers rather than needles to stimulate them.

There are different theories as to how acupuncture works. Scientific theory believes that it

Above and right: Here we see Qigong exercises for bringing energy into the spleen (top left) and into the heart and lungs (above and right).

helps to release endorphins – the body's natural pain relievers – but this represents only one aspect of acupuncture and doesn't explain how it successfully treats chronic illness nor how it operates holistically. The Chinese philosophy underpinning acupuncture adopts a Mind/Body approach. It is believed that physical illness upsets the mind and that emotional or mental upset affects the organs. So, for example, someone who worries excessively may develop stomach ulcers, because that type of mental activity affects the stomach. Therefore, in making a diagnosis the acupuncturist will assess both the physical and emotional symptoms in order to obtain a holistic overview of the disease pattern. The way in which acupuncture then works to resolve an imbalance in the energy system is very similar to Reiki, but what differentiates them is the method by which the energy is rebalanced and the fact that acupuncturists make diagnoses.

Reflexology

Reflexology has become extremely popular in spite of the common reaction to it – that it is impossible to treat the whole body just by working on the feet. Although reflexology was known in several ancient civilizations, it was only developed as a therapy in the 1960s by Dr William Fitzgerald, an American doctor, who called it 'zone therapy'. Fitzgerald divided the body into 10 zones and found that by applying pressure on the body in one part of the zone (feet or hands) he could relieve pain in other parts of the same zone. But it was not until a physiotherapist called Eunice Ingham mapped the charts of the feet's reflex zones that it was known as reflexology.

The idea of specific points on the foot corresponding to

particular organs is very similar to the meridian system, and the way in which a reflexology treatment is given is acupressure, using the fingers, but concentrating only on the feet. As with the other therapies discussed here, the practitioner is looking for energy blocks that they then work to release. Most reflexologists are not trained medically, so they do not diagnose, although they must be able to recognize where there are blockages. This can supplement an existing medical diagnosis, as a doctor may recommend reflexology for arthritis but not realize that there is also a block in the kidney energy.

One benefit of reflexology is that, like Reiki, it can be self-administered. Most of us do not take good care of our feet and yet

Below and right: Reflexologists base their treatment on stimulating nerve endings in specific areas of the left and right foot that correspond to specific areas in other parts of the body. By doing so they attempt to influence body systems that will lead to improvement in health and well being. The illustration below gives some idea of how a foot chart is laid out.

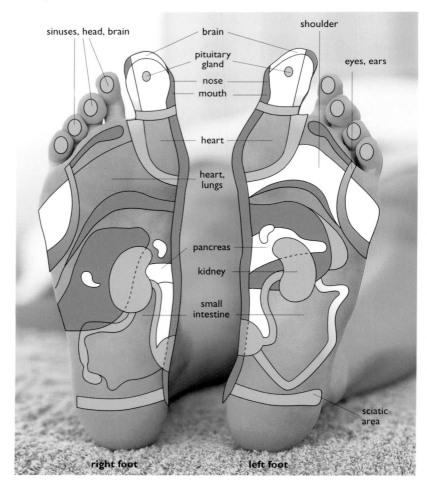

sinuses, head, brain
brain
shoulder
pituitary gland
eyes, ears
nose
mouth
heart
heart, lungs
pancreas
kidney
small intestine
sciatic area
right foot   **left foot**

to take it gently and not to keep pressing for long periods of time on the points that are painful. It is tempting to think that if you keep pressing on an acupoint you will speed up the healing, but in my experience it doesn't work like that; it is better to apply a light amount of pressure for a short time each day. As a Reiki practitioner, this is a way to help you maintain your own health and advance your holistic understanding of the body. Additionally, it is something that you can pass on to your clients so that they can experiment with ways of helping themselves, as anything that empowers them to do so will result in faster healing.

Bach flower remedies

These are distinctly different from all the previously mentioned therapies, but a knowledge of them is useful to all therapists. There are a number of other flower essences available now, but the Bach range is the most widely accessible and is sold in chemists as well as in health food shops.

The Bach flower remedies consist of 38 tinctures, the most widely known one being Rescue Remedy. They were created by Dr Edward Bach, who trained as a physician and a homoeopath. While working at the Royal London Homoeopathic Hospital he developed his understanding of vibrational healing and found that patients with the same emotional difficulties could be helped with the same homeopathic remedy, even if they were manifesting very different physical symptoms. He developed the flower remedies from observing that the early-morning dew on plants absorbed some of the plant's properties. He conducted extensive tests until he arrived at 38 remedies, which he believed would heal all personalities and emotional states.

they are probably one of the most stressed parts of the body. You should give yourself a reflexology massage in the evenings, after soaking your feet in warm water and using almond oil (or an oil of your choice) with a few drops of lavender oil blended in. This will not only make you ready for a good night's sleep, but it will also help to keep your feet in good shape and enable you to become aware of which parts of your body need more energy. It is important

He classified these emotional states into seven major groups: fear, uncertainty, loneliness, oversensitivity, despondency, over-concern for the welfare of others and insufficient interest in present circumstances. The tinctures contain the energetic qualities of the plant and act at the level of the emotions to produce healing. The flower remedies are very safe and easy to use as the drops can be placed directly on the tongue or in water. The remedies are usually taken four times a day and the length of time they are taken for is up to the individual, as each of us takes a different amount of time to resolve the problem.

It is a good idea for all households to keep a bottle of Rescue Remedy for when there are sudden emotional upsets. Reiki practitioners who have taken the Second Degree (see page 56) will have the extra tools needed to use Reiki in working directly on the emotions, and I would definitely recommend that they too keep a bottle of Rescue Remedy at hand in case a client has an emotional crisis during or after a treatment.

The Bach Centre that makes the flower remedies produces a very useful wall chart relating each essence to the particular emotional states. To find out which remedy I or other people need, I lay the chart out flat and use a pendulum to dowse it for the most appropriate one, or in some cases a combination of two or three. As with the other therapies described here, you need to study a specialist book to learn about the treatment in depth.

Case study

A woman to whom I had given Reiki treatments previously asked if she could have another course of treatments. She didn't feel there was anything specifically wrong with her, other than exhaustion from overwork. That she was physically tired was apparent in the first session, as her body was drawing in large amounts of energy (this is often the case in first sessions). In the second session, my attention was drawn to her mental exhaustion and to the overactivity of her brain. As the woman is a therapist herself, this was explained by the fact that she had just come from an intensive session with one of her clients. After four more sessions there was an improvement in her overall energy levels, but I intuitively felt during the last session that what she really needed was to use her own body to combat the tiredness. At the end of the treatment, while we were discussing how she felt, I suggested that she tried Qigong to counterbalance the amount of mental activity in her life. She seemed quite surprised and told me that she had practised T'ai Chi, a related therapy, in the past and that a day or so before she came to see me she had been considering taking it up again. The message I intuited from her energy while giving her Reiki reinforced her own conscious knowledge about what she needed to do, making it easier for her to decide to find a class.

Below and left: One method of extracting the flower remedies involves placing the appropriate flowers in a glass bowl filled with Spring water. The bowl is then placed in sunlight for several hours to allow the plant to energize the water.

preparing for reiki

There are three aspects to this: preparing yourself to receive the Reiki attunements, preparing yourself to give a Reiki treatment and preparing a room or space in which to give a Reiki treatment.

Preparing for the Reiki attunements

Once you have decided to receive the attunements of the First Degree (see page 54) in Reiki and have found a Reiki Master, it is

Above: Simply drinking plenty of water can help your system to cleanse itself in preparation for receiving the Reiki attunements.
Right: If you practise yoga, it can be helpful to sit calmly in the lotus position for a short while in preparation for giving a Reiki treatment.

likely that you will be asked to make some small preparations before the course. The first is to try to eat as healthfully as possible for several days before. Food is a major source of our energy and the better the quality of food we eat, the better the quality of energy we have available to us. Home-cooked food using organic products is the best for this. Drinking plenty of spring water can also help to cleanse the system. You will be asked to abstain from drinking alcohol for at least the preceding two or three days. Alcohol and other substances that alter consciousness block the flow of energy through the body. As you are about to receive attunements that will cause a sudden surge of energy, it is best to be in as strong a state as possible. However, it is not necessary to attempt a full body detox. Similarly, once you are practising Reiki, you should never give a treatment if you have been drinking alcohol. It won't do the other person any harm, but as the Reiki comes through you it may cause you to have some unpleasant reactions. It is unlikely that most people would think of giving Reiki after drinking, but in the first flush of enthusiasm about the therapy, there can be a desire to give treatments to everyone, everywhere, even at parties.

Preparing yourself to give a Reiki treatment

These are simple and, probably, obvious preparations. Ideally, your clothes should not smell of cooking or smoke. Also, try to avoid eating too much garlic before giving a treatment as it's the kind of smell that can interfere with a client's comfort. Similarly, don't

wear strong perfumes, though you can rub an aromatherapy oil (blended with a base oil) on your hands if you think it adds to the treatment. I like to wash my hands before starting a treatment and rub a little rose oil into them because I associate 'rose' with opening the heart chakra. I also remove any jewellery I am wearing, such as rings, bracelets and watch, as it can get in the way of the treatment and possibly scratch the client. I sit quietly for a few minutes before the client arrives, at the same time giving Reiki to myself, usually in the heart and solar plexus area. I might also do the grounding exercise below.

When the treatment is over it is important to disconnect yourself from the other person's energy body. The simplest way to do this is by washing your hands immediately and acknowledging to yourself that the treatment is finished. You may devise other rituals, although you should always include washing your hands.

Grounding exercise

Sitting on a chair with your spine straight, visualize a rope descending from the tail of your spine. See it go through the floor, down through the earth, then the layers of rock, until you feel that you are near the centre of the earth, then anchor the rope there. You can also visualize your body going through the earth with the rope and, having anchored it, come back to your sitting position.

Now imagine that there are two holes in the bottom of your feet and that a heavy brownish-red warm sludge is coming up through these holes and circulating throughout your lower body. Do this until your lower body feels heavier. Then visualize a distant point in the heavens from which a beam of white light is coming down to connect with a point on the crown of your head. Feel the white light flow through this point into your head and through the upper part of your body, cleansing it and making it feel lighter.

Now feel the two different energies circulating at the same time and finish the exercise by touching the floor with your hands to allow any excess energy to return to the earth. This exercise takes only a few minutes to do. As with all visualization exercises, don't become obsessed with trying to see everything clearly — forming the idea in your mind is enough to make it work.

Preparing a room and your equipment

Ideally you should use a massage table for giving treatments. If you don't have one you can use a bed or put a duvet on the floor and work there, but only do this if you are giving treatments infrequently or you will end up with back problems. If you are using a table, cover it with a sheet or specially made massage table cover and place a small towel where the client's head will be. You will also need a blanket to cover the client as the body quickly becomes cold when it is in a relaxed state. Keep a box of tissues near the table, as tears sometimes flow during Reiki treatments when old hurts surface.

If you are working from home, choose the room that you feel will be most relaxing for giving treatments and prepare it with care and respect. It's best to have a room that you use only for Reiki, but it is more important that whatever room you use is clean, quiet, warm and comfortable. Air it well before the treatment and burn some incense before the treatment rather than during it, as some people, particularly those with bronchial problems, are irritated by it. Alternatively you can scent the room with an oil burner, using an oil that promotes relaxation. Salt is good for clearing your environment — some people throw salt into the four corners of a room or simply keep a bowl of salt in the room.

I like to have music playing while I give a treatment, but I make sure the volume is fairly low, as otherwise it is too obtrusive. There are some albums specifically aimed at Reiki practitioners that include a bell ringing when it is time to change hand positions. You might find these useful at first, but I find them lacking musically and instead prefer to use melodic, relaxing and non-energizing music.

Above: Scattering salt in the four corners of a room can be a good means of cleansing the surrounding energy in preparation for giving a treatment.
Left: It is important to wash your hands immediately after giving a Reiki treatment in order to disconnect yourself from your client's energy.

ways of using reiki

Apart from self-treatments and treating others, Reiki can be used for a number of other purposes. This makes it quite distinct from other healing methods as it really can be utilized in all aspects of daily life. Most of the examples given here can be employed by all levels of Reiki practitioners, except for the distance healing method (see page 38), which is only available to those who have taken the Second Degree (see page 56).

In the world of scientific materialism, many people find it hard to believe that Reiki can be used on, for example, inanimate objects, and even those who are practising Reiki can sometimes find it difficult to take in. In this case experience provides the proof, so when you have a problem with your computer or one of your plants is dying, try Reiki, remembering that everything in the universe is created from energy and that all you are doing is giving energy where there is a lack or imbalance.

Plants and flowers
Life energy is as much a part of vegetation as it is of humans and animals. There are a number of ways in which Reiki can enhance the life of your plants.

With indoor plants, begin by giving Reiki to the roots by placing your hands around the pot. If you think of a plant as having a body, this is the area of the plant that takes in the sustenance that keeps it alive, so it is more important to give Reiki to the roots than to the upper part of the plant. When you intuitively feel that enough energy has been drawn into the roots, move your hands to the upper body of the plant and, holding your hands about 2.5 cm/1 inch away from the leaves, give Reiki again. Obviously, you also need to attend to the plant in the normal way – Reiki will not be able to help if the plant also needs to be repotted. If a house plant is not doing well in spite of all your care and giving it Reiki, try moving it to another part of the room. Plants are good indicators of negative energy caused by geopathic stress areas – such as underground streams or ley lines – under a building, and they will often thrive when they are moved, regardless of light conditions.

You can also give Reiki to your garden or to individual garden plants. If you are planting bedding plants or growing flowers or vegetables from seed, give Reiki to them before planting. If you have a large garden it is probably impossible for you to give Reiki to everything, but if you have Second Degree Reiki then you can use the method for distance healing to send Reiki to your entire garden. Whatever the level of your gardening skills, or your Reiki, you can experiment with using Reiki on plants until you find the method that works best for you.

Food and drink
Like plants, food contains life energy. Food gives its energy to us and we in turn utilize it through the metabolic process. Therefore, the higher the quality of energy in the food we eat, the better the energy we have available. Some food has more energy to start with – organic, fresh, raw food has the most, while processed food has the least. Very few of us want to live on wheatgrass juice and raw carrot all the time, even if we are health conscious, but with Reiki you can even improve the quality of energy in a sticky toffee pudding. You can give Reiki to your food while it is cooking, by holding your hands above the saucepan. Alternatively, you can give Reiki to food once it is on the plate. This method can be used at home, and also when you are eating out, as you can energize your food by discreetly holding your hands at either side of your plate, palms facing in, rather than above it.

Above: Reiki can be used to give energy to a number of inanimate objects. Giving Reiki to the food you eat could help to increase its nutritional value.
Right: If a house plant is failing to thrive, try giving Reiki to the roots and then to the upper body.

The same principle can be applied to liquids, particularly to water and alcohol. During my First Degree Reiki (see page 54), the Reiki Master asked each of us to hold a glass of London tap water and give it Reiki for a few minutes, then taste it and see if we could tell the difference. It definitely tasted sweeter and cleaner than usual. If you have a bottle of wine that tastes slightly acid on opening, give the bottle Reiki for a few minutes and it will improve the taste. You can do this with hot drinks as well.

Animals

Sick or distressed animals respond very positively to Reiki and generally they relax very quickly. Since animals are more instinctive than we are, they are more able to judge how much Reiki they need and how often they need it.

The procedure for treating animals is not very different to that for treating humans, although as they cannot verbally communicate you will need to be guided more by your intuition and observation, which includes being guided by the animal itself. Animal's organs are in much the same position as ours and you should try to cover all the main ones. A good technique is to start with your hands behind the animal's ears, as this seems to calm most of them down. Animals require different techniques according to size: a hamster can be cupped in your hands, fish can be treated by placing your hands on the fish tank, while animals you prefer not to touch can be treated using the distance method.

Environment

At home, after physically cleaning the rooms, it is a good idea to give the energy in each room a clean too. To do this, draw the first symbol given at the Second Degree in each corner of the room. You might also try burning Native American smudge sticks, available at New Age shops, around the house. (Smudge can also be used to clean the aura of a person. To do this brush the smoke with a feather, in an upward movement, around the whole body (see page 124). If you also do this in your office or in meeting rooms before your colleagues arrive, you will all benefit from a sense of increased harmony and find a decrease in difficulties at work.)

If you don't have the Second Degree, I suggest you use intention and visualization to give Reiki to a room. You could also try putting your hands on the walls. In my First Degree class there was a woman who had been trying to sell her house for some time. After finishing the course she went home and decided to give Reiki to all the walls of her house – and she had a buyer within two weeks. You can also give Reiki to household appliances to ensure they continue to work well, and there are stories of people using Reiki to fix computer and car problems. All degree levels can do all this.

Distance healing

Distance or absent healing is not unique to Reiki, although the method used is. Intellectually, distance healing is problematic; it is difficult for some people to believe that it is possible to send healing energy over thousands of miles to another person or to a situation such as civil war or famine, while others accept it instinctively.

Just as I cannot say exactly how prayers are answered, I cannot describe the mechanisms of

Above: Reiki can be used for a number of purposes, include treating domestic pets who respond very well to Reiki.
Right: You can use Reiki to cleanse the energy in your environment, whether at work or at home, by simply putting your hands on the walls.

distance healing definitively. However, I believe that everything in the universe has one origin and that consequently every thing and every person is interconnected. This makes it possible for us all to connect beyond the physical plane. Some describe this as a connection at the level of the heart. Reiki practitioners use symbols and visualization techniques that include the use of photographs to make this heart connection and there are examples throughout this book of the circumstances in which it can be used.

You can also use distance healing to send Reiki to your past and future. When sending it to the past, visualize yourself at a point in your life or use an old photograph of yourself. Hold the photograph in your receiving hand and draw the distance healing symbol given at the Second Degree with your giving hand, then cover it with that same hand. (It is generally accepted that the receiving hand is the left and the giving hand the right, because energy flows down the right side of the body and comes up the left.) The same technique can heal past relationships, using a photograph or visualizing the other person.

Sending Reiki to your future can support the use of positive affirmations and the type of visualization as taught by Shakti Gawain in her book *Creative Visualization*. Draw the distance healing symbol on the palm of your left hand while visualizing what you want to manifest in your future. If you don't have Second Degree Reiki, write what you want on a piece of paper and give Reiki to it. In either method you should be clear about what you want and state it positively: never say 'I don't want', always 'I want'. Whatever you ask for, it must not harm another person. Also, be open. If you want a new relationship, don't specify the person you want to have a relationship with, just ask for the best relationship for you. When I visualize something I want, I always add these words at the end, 'This, or something better now manifests for me in totally satisfying and harmonious ways for the highest good of all concerned.'

medical questions

Reiki does not require you to take down a medical history, as you are not going to make a diagnosis. It is, however, vital to ask a person who wants to receive Reiki if they have a pacemaker or diabetes.

For those with a pacemaker, I would recommend extreme caution. While Reiki is essentially very safe, the effect of the Reiki energy on such a device is unpredictable. It is never pleasant to refuse someone a Reiki treatment and you will have to handle such a situation with sensitivity, explaining to them that it is for their benefit that you don't want to take the risk.

With regard to diabetes, Reiki is known to affect the levels of insulin required in the body, usually by reducing the dosage, and if the person is not aware of this they could be giving themselves too much insulin. You will need to talk to them about the way they handle their diabetes and you should know something about the two basic ways in which it is controlled by clinicians. In Type I diabetes, insulin levels are low or non-existent, forcing the body to obtain energy from body fat. This type of diabetes is most common in those under 35 and has to be treated with insulin, otherwise the result is a diabetic coma leading to death. Type II diabetes most often manifests in people over 40 and as its onset is slower it can go undiagnosed for a long period.

This type of diabetes can be treated by changes in diet and oral medication. Therefore, it is important to establish what type of diabetes a person has. If they are insulin-dependent, they probably measure their insulin levels daily. You must tell them that if they want to receive Reiki they must monitor their insulin requirements very carefully. If you and they feel confident they can do this then you can continue. Restate this at the end of the session and make a follow-up telephone call to them within a day or two to see if they have experienced any difference. The most important thing to remember is that if you do not feel comfortable about treating someone with this condition, don't do it – Reiki practitioners are not clinically trained and you don't want to leave yourself open to legal action.

This leads us to the question of insurance for professional liability. There are a number of insurance companies that offer cover for Reiki practitioners but it is a rather vexed area, as Reiki is seen as providing its own protection for the giver and receiver, so worldly things such as insurance should not be necessary. However, consider the possible repercussions if someone falls off the treatment table or trips over your doorstep. If you are practising on a regular basis it is advisable to consider insurance. Complementary health magazines carry advertisements from insurance companies offering suitable policies. It is also worthwhile contacting the Reiki Association as they will probably be able to provide a list of recommended insurers.

Finally, although it is not necessary to take a full medical

history, you will need to discuss with your client the reason they have come to see you. If it is for a physical condition, establish the way in which they have been treated to date, including their use of other complementary therapies and the results. If possible, establish this briefly when they make the appointment so that you can do some research before their first session, then go into more detail with them when you meet them. If they want treatment for a mental/emotional condition, find out if they are on medication and research the effects of that drug. There are good guides to medicines for lay people and it is worth getting one. I'm sure that there are many Reiki practitioners who feel that this is completely unnecessary, but your extra knowledge will help you to empathize with your client, while still allowing Reiki to do its work in an open way. You must never recommend that a person stops taking their medication, or advise altering the dosage in any way.

the historical and spiritual principles

Reiki is not only a healing method – it also provides a method for developing yourself spiritually, although this aspect is often under-emphasized. I believe that this is the result of a radical swing towards a culture where everyone wants to be a 'healer' and where Reiki is perceived of as a 'fast' method of performing healing miracles. We have always needed to explore our potential as healers and we will continue to need to do this, but this has to be done in the context of exploring our whole selves. We can use Reiki as one way to do this. It does not require ascetic practice, just the integration of Reiki into daily life. By also contemplating the spiritual principles as laid down by Dr Usui we find that Reiki leads us to a different understanding of ourselves and others, gradually clearing away old habits and attitudes, and enabling us to see everything in a more positive light.

'Reiki is not just another therapy, although it is, without doubt, highly therapeutic. It offers itself as a spiritual discipline and pathway. From the moment on the top of a mountain in Japan when Reiki exploded onto the earth through the experience of Dr Usui, it has challenged us by asking "More than anything else, more, perhaps, even than life itself, what is it that you want?" Reiki asks us whether we are willing to give our all in exchange for all that we would wish to receive. The question is, can we give what it takes?'

Reiki Master **Don Alexander**

the story of the three masters

One of the traditions of Reiki is the telling of the story of its rediscovery by Dr Mikao Usui. Initially I saw this story as a factual history, but I now believe it combines historical characters with symbolic spiritual elements, the meaning of which must be sought out over time. In this way it bears similarities to the stories of the quest for the Holy Grail in the Western tradition.

The story is part of an oral tradition, although you will find a version of the story in all books on Reiki. By oral tradition, I mean that the Reiki Master will tell the story to their students as they themselves have been taught it, rather than referring to a standardized written version. In telling the story, the Master will emphasize different aspects of it and will invite their students to contemplate the elements that they believe to be important for their understanding of Reiki. This imbues a story that is not simply a factual history with personal belief and is the reason why there are so many versions, each of them slightly different. As with all storytelling, some versions are more satisfying than others, but when we choose a Master we also choose the story we will hear. Afterwards we can create our own story based on our own experience of Reiki. The story as written in this book is my own version of it.

Dr Mikao Usui

Dr Usui lived in the city of Kyoto, Japan, in the second half of the 19th century. This was a time of great change in Japan and the country had recently become more open to foreigners. As a result, many Christian missionaries came there. Dr Usui, although originally probably a follower of Shintoism and Buddhism in the Japanese style, had fully embraced Christianity, and had become a minister as well as a teacher at a Christian college for boys in Kyoto. During one of his classes, his students asked him if he believed literally in the Bible. Dr Usui replied that he did. His students then asked him how he explained the miracle healings by Jesus and His instructions to the apostles to heal the sick and raise the dead. They also asked him what Jesus had meant when He said, 'You will do as I have done and even greater things.' If this were true, they reasoned with Dr Usui, the world should be full of healers.

Dr Usui had no answer for his students, but he felt personally challenged to go out and find one. He resigned his position at the college and set about discovering the way in which Jesus healed the sick. Because Western missionaries had taught him and Christianity is considered to be a Western religion, he decided that the West was where he should look first, and he set off for the USA, where he lived for seven years. He enrolled at a theological college in Chicago, studying comparative religion, and it was there that he learned to read Sanskrit, the ancient language of India and Tibet, and of many religious texts. But he did not find the answers he was looking for.

He decided to return to Japan, thinking that in the Japanese Lotus sutras he might find information about the method of healing used by the Buddha. He travelled around many Buddhist monasteries asking the monks if they had information about the Buddha's method of physical healing. Although it was accepted that the Buddha had performed healing, the practice of Buddhism had moved its focus entirely to healing the spirit, and so none of the monks that Dr Usui approached could help him. Finally he approached a Zen monastery where the abbot agreed with him that it must be possible to heal the body as the Buddha had done, but that during the centuries of concentration on healing the spirit the method had been lost. Greatly encouraged, Dr Usui stayed at the monastery, where he studied the Japanese

Buddhist sutras in the original Sanskrit. Although he found texts that described the method of healing, he still lacked the information that would enable him to activate the energy and use it himself.

Dr Usui then concluded that he might gain more information if he travelled to Tibet and studied the Tibetan Buddhist sutras. In the 19th century, scrolls had been found in Tibet that documented the travels in the Himalayas of a St Isa, who is thought by many to be Jesus. There is no evidence that Dr Usui read these scrolls. However, it is known that after he completed his study of the Tibetan Buddhist sutras he felt he had found all the intellectual answers, but still did not have the means of activating the energy. He returned to Japan and to the Zen monastery and, after discussing it with the abbot, who encouraged him in his quest, decided that he should go on a retreat for a 21-day fast and meditation.

The place Dr Usui and the abbot chose for the retreat was Mount Kuri Yama, a sacred mountain not far from Kyoto. Having climbed to a spot facing east, Dr Usui collected 21 stones in a pile to serve as his calendar,

Left: Dr Mikao Usui, the first Grand Master, rediscovered Reiki in the second half of the 19th century.

Below: Some people like to prepare a space in their homes which they use for meditation or contemplation. Candles or simple natural objects such as plants, flowers or stones can help to create a sacred space.

intending to throw away a stone at the end of every day. In the time just before dawn on his twenty-first day, which was very dark as it was the new moon, he felt for his last stone, and as he did so he prayed for an answer to come. At that moment he saw a light hurtling towards him across the sky. As it got closer to him it became larger and at first he was afraid and wanted to run away from it. But he decided to accept whatever it would bring him, even if it was death, and as he faced it the light struck him in the Third Eye (Sixth *Chakra*) in the centre of his forehead. Millions of rainbow-coloured bubbles appeared before his eyes and in them he saw the Reiki symbols. As he saw the symbols he was given information about each one and its use in activating the healing energy. Reiki had now been rediscovered.

When Dr Usui came out of his trance-like state he found it was broad daylight. He started to run down the mountain to share his discovery with the abbot at the Zen monastery and, in his haste, he tripped on a stone and stubbed his toe. He bent down to hold his toe and was amazed when after a few minutes the bleeding stopped and the toe was completely healed. This was the first miracle. As he came to the bottom of the mountain, he found a roadside eating place and ordered a full breakfast. The proprietor could see that he had been on a long fast, and knowing that it was dangerous to eat a large amount after a fast, he tried to persuade Dr Usui to have something lighter. Dr Usui declined and ate the large breakfast without getting indigestion. This was the second miracle. The proprietor's granddaughter, who had been serving Dr Usui, was in great pain, as she had been suffering for days with toothache and a swollen jaw

and her grandfather was too poor to take her to a dentist. Dr Usui offered to help and she accepted. After he had put his hands on both sides of her face the pain disappeared. This was the third miracle. Dr Usui then continued his journey to the monastery, where he found the abbot in a great deal of arthritic pain. While he told the abbot about his experiences he laid his hands on the arthritic areas and again the pain disappeared. This was the fourth miracle of the day.

Now Dr Usui had to decide how to use this newly found power and after meditation and after consultation with the abbot he chose to work in the Beggars' Quarter of Kyoto. He lived there for seven years, healing people every day and urging them to start a new life, but he found that many of the people he healed returned to begging. He asked one man why he had done so, and the man told him that although he had found a job and had got married after his healing, he could not handle being responsible for his own life, and so he preferred to be a beggar.

Dr Usui, discouraged by this attitude, then left the Beggars' Quarter and travelled throughout Japan teaching Reiki. He now realized that he could use the Reiki symbols he had been given to attune others so that they could also give Reiki and take responsibility for their own lives. It was also at this time that he started to train other men as Masters, one of them being Chujiro Hayashi, who would become Dr Usui's successor and be responsible for carrying on the traditions of Reiki.

Dr Chujiro Hayashi and Mrs Hawayo Takata

Chujiro Hayashi was a retired naval officer who, following Dr Usui's teachings, founded a Reiki clinic in

Above: Dr Chujiro Hayashi followed the teachings of Dr Usui and opened a clinic in Tokyo.
Right: Hawayo Takata came to Dr Hayashi's clinic in 1935 and was eventually named by Dr Hayashi as his successor, responsible for continuing the traditions of Reiki.
Far right: Phyllis Furumoto, the granddaughter of Hawayo Takata, is recognised by many Reiki Masters as the current Grand Master.

Tokyo and trained many in the use of Reiki. In his clinic healers worked in groups on people and also went to their homes if they were not able to attend. Not much is known about Dr Hayashi, although new material coming out of Japan now suggests that, like Dr Usui, he created many Reiki Masters. However, his spiritual or psychic abilities were at the time critical to the survival of Reiki, and it was to his clinic that Hawayo Takata came to be cured.

Hawayo Takata was born in 1900 on the Hawaiian island of Kauai. In 1935, after having been married and widowed and with two small daughters, she developed nervous exhaustion accompanied by a physical illness and was told that she required an operation to save her life. While on a visit to Japan to see her parents, she went to a hospital for the surgery. On the day of the operation, while she was being prepared for the anaesthetic, she heard a voice tell her, 'The operation is not necessary.' She spoke to her doctor about her reservations and asked him if there was another way that she could be healed. The doctor said that he knew of a place in Tokyo that she could go to if she could stay in Japan for a longer period of time. The doctor was aware of Reiki because his sister had been healed by it and had herself become a practitioner. And so it was that Hawayo Takata arrived at Dr Hayashi's Reiki clinic, where she received treatment and was cured.

After staying at the clinic for some months, she asked Dr Hayashi if he would teach her Reiki. At first he refused because she was a foreigner and he was concerned about Reiki leaving Japan in its early days. However, Mrs Takata persevered and was initiated in the First and Second Degrees (see pages 54 and 56) before returning to Hawaii, where she began her own practice. In

1938, about a year after she had gone back to Hawaii, Dr Hayashi visited her, initiated her as a Reiki Master and then announced that she was to be his successor with the responsibility for carrying on the traditions of Reiki. He also told her that whenever he summoned her to Japan she must come immediately.

Dr Hayashi had powerful psychic abilities and he foresaw that Japan and America were going to be at war with each other in the near future. He also knew what the result of the war would be for Japan. He sent for Mrs Takata to come to Tokyo, and when she arrived he told her what was going to happen and what she must do to preserve Reiki. As he had previously been a naval officer he was also afraid that he might be drafted into military service and this was now against his principles. Therefore, in full ceremonial dress and with all his family and friends around him, Chujiro Hayashi consciously left his body.

Mrs Takata returned to Hawaii and somehow managed to escape being incarcerated as a Japanese-American during the war. Finally she brought Reiki to mainland America. During the last 10 years of her life (she died on 11 December 1980), she initiated 22 Reiki Masters who would spread Reiki throughout America, Europe and the rest of the world. She also named her granddaughter, Phyllis Lei Furumoto, as her successor, and she is currently recognized by many Reiki Masters as the Grand Master.

There are many variations on this story, and there are doubtless many questions that people have about the gaps in it, but, as in a fairy story, it is the inner meaning, which is liable to individual interpretation, rather than the logical consistency that really matters here.

reiki in the present
– differences and diversions

Those readers who practise Reiki cannot help but have noticed that a debate has developed recently about the way Reiki is taught and practised. This has led to some Reiki Masters being antagonistic towards the methods of others and to claims being made about what is the 'real Reiki'. Those of you who use the Internet will find the various arguments being debated, sometimes aggressively, in the Reiki newsgroups.

The history of the debate, in the UK at least, is that until a few years ago there was only a handful of Reiki Masters in the country. Most, if not all, of these Masters belong to the Reiki Alliance headed by Phyllis Furumoto. While they were away at a Masters' conference, two independent Masters came to England, and within just a few days created something in the region of 70 new Reiki Masters. These new Masters in turn created more and so on. Out of this arose two core issues of the debate: one is the speed of initiating people through the Degrees and the other is payment. There are other issues that have arisen as the debate has developed internationally, the main one being the presentation of the Reiki symbols in a book. (They can now also be found on the Internet.)

Within the traditional system, prescribed periods of time are recommended between the attunements, the minimum period between the First and the Second Degrees (see pages 54 and 56) being three months. Only one or two people at a time are carefully selected by a Master to be trained as a Master and this training usually lasts approximately a year. However, the independent Reiki Masters were sometimes offering both degrees and even creating Masters all in the same weekend. On top of this there is the issue of money, with the non-traditional teachers charging a lower price than the traditional teachers.

Without finding it necessary to take sides, I see Reiki as an evolving practice. Dr Usui rediscovered it and with spiritual guidance devised and refined the form as far as he could within his lifetime. He then handed it on to his successor, Dr Hayashi, who with his clinic had the opportunity to work with Reiki in a different setting and to refine it further according to his spiritual guidance. Mrs Takata, while still working with the basic practice that she learned, will as an individual have imprinted her own experience on the way she taught it, and in fact it is her hand positions for the body treatment that are most widely used today. But even these vary between Masters of the Takata lineage, leading one to wonder if she taught all her students exactly the same methods.

If you consider psychoanalysis, Freud discovered it and devised the basic method, but his work is not the totality of the form; rather, it only represents the beginning. Psychoanalysis is constantly evolving. The work of Jung

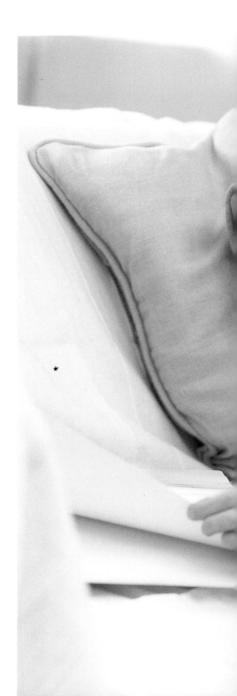

represents the first real breakaway from Freud's thinking, but it is still considered to be within the psychoanalytic tradition, even if Freudians do not agree with it. It is a matter of personal belief for each analyst as to which school they follow. Today, psychoanalysts of all schools do not base their entire working methods solely on the methods of the founders, but have added into their methodology all the work that has been done since.

This example illustrates that nothing stands still – not an intellectual discipline, nor a religion or healing method. There are always new discoveries and new ways of working. Both sides in the debate have some very convincing arguments for their position, but I feel that the choice of path to take with Reiki is an individual matter, and that everyone should feel free to use whatever suits them best without condemnation.

the spiritual principles

The Five Spiritual Principles of Reiki were laid down by Dr Usui after he had been working in the Beggars' Quarter. Some sources say that he took them from guidelines for living a fulfilled life set down by the Meiji Emperor of Japan (1868–1912), while others believe that they reflect Dr Usui's Christian beliefs. Whatever the source, they are the result of Dr Usui's observations of human nature and the necessity of us all taking responsibility for our own lives in order to achieve healing at all levels. He felt that people needed guidelines to help them take that responsibility in all their life situations. For someone who is fully in connection with life, following the Five Spiritual Principles will be as effortless as breathing. However, most of us are not in that state and we need aids to get us there. Reciting the Principles to yourself daily or making an effort to follow at least one of them throughout the day will have remarkable and positive effects on your consciousness, as Dr Usui intended. As with other things in Reiki, you will find some variation in the Principles taught by each Master.

Just for today do not worry

When we worry we have lost faith. We are no longer able to see the 'big picture' or trust in what is happening to us. We worry about the future and try to control it in order to protect ourselves from pain, instead of allowing it to unfold gracefully and experiencing even greater things than we could imagine for ourselves. Mostly we worry because we don't believe that the world is full of abundance and we feel we will have to fight for everything we want. Choose something that is a worry for you, and just for today don't worry about it. Ask the divine for help with it instead, and have faith that when you ask you will be answered.

Just for today do not anger

Anger mostly arises out of the feeling that you have lost control; when you become angry with someone you feel that you will regain it. If you observe your anger as it arises you will see that it reflects something about you that needs attention, rather than a shortcoming in the person with whom you are angry. Other people we draw into our sphere are our mirrors, so look carefully at those who annoy you the most, as they reflect aspects of yourself you would rather not see. Become an observer of your anger before you express it and then you will realize there isn't anything to be angry about.

Honour your parents, teachers and elders

We should show respect for those who gave us life. Even if our relationship with them is not good, we should adopt a positive attitude of respect because then there is a better chance of resolving the negative feelings on either side. Also, many people are our teachers; they may be younger or older than us, but it is important to acknowledge teaching when we receive it, if only inwardly.

Earn your living honestly

This probably comes directly from Dr Usui's experience in the Beggars' Quarter. Supporting ourselves honestly is a way of reinforcing our taking responsibility for our own lives.

Show gratitude to everything

Although we are all co-creators in the universe, we are not the ultimate source. Affirming gratitude to the source of creation for everything we have, no matter how mundane, is a way of reinforcing our feeling of being blessed with abundance, and from this more abundance flows.

reiki initiations – first degree reiki

Reiki initiations are divided into three Degrees, the Third (see page 58) being the initiation as a Reiki Master. On one level this is because a new student cannot be expected to assimilate advanced teaching while still learning the basics. On another it relates to the fact that the attunements expand the person's vibratory rate and amplify the amount of energy that the body can channel through it. Therefore, if all the attunements were done at the same time, the person receiving them might become like an overloaded electrical socket and have a blowout. By taking it in stages, the physical and etheric bodies, including the *chakra* system, are able to rebalance gradually after each attunement level. However, everyone has their own reaction to the attunements, and people who have already been involved in other types of energy work will probably respond to them in a different way to those who have not.

What happens in a First Degree Reiki class will vary from teacher to teacher; even the way the attunements are given will differ according to which tradition the teacher comes from. However, the Reiki Master will usually allow the class to progress according to the needs of the group.

The day will usually begin with everyone introducing themselves and saying what led them to Reiki. The Reiki Master will then often tell the story of their own path with Reiki and describe its history. This is followed by the first attunement, which each person receives individually.

From this first attunement most people feel the energy flowing through their hands. Some people also feel the presence of spirits, while others see vivid colours or experience intense feelings of love. Afterwards everyone should have time to discuss what they have experienced. After a break, the second attunement will be given and the Master will show the hand positions for self-treatment and for treating others. If the course is held over two days, as is usual, the third and fourth attunements will be given the next day. At the end of the first day, most people feel rather 'spacey'. It is advisable to rest that evening.

The second day might begin with everyone recounting their experience since the previous day's class before moving on to the third attunement. Most of the rest of the day will be spent on everyone giving treatments to each other, so that the Reiki Master is sure everyone knows the positions and understands their purpose. Some Reiki Masters do give their classes basic handouts showing the hand positions so that students can refer to them at home. There might also be some discussion of other ways of using Reiki, such as with food, but again this varies; I have found that while some Masters go into extensive discussions of the many ways in which Reiki can be used, others barely mention it. Finally, the last attunement will be given. This grounds the energy and seals it in permanently (and gets rid of the spacey feeling) so that for the rest of your life you will be able to channel the Reiki energy, even if you don't use it for a long time.

Following the attunements it is traditional for all students to give themselves a Reiki treatment every day for 21 days. This symbolically represents the time Dr Usui spent fasting and meditating, but it is also the amount of time it takes the new energy to move through each of the seven *chakras* and basically settle down. During that time many old negative emotions and physical ailments may surface as the vibratory rate of the body changes. By giving yourself a Reiki treatment every day you both ease the pain of this process and speed it up. It is beneficial to keep a daily Reiki journal during this period as doing this allows you to examine and express your feelings in a concrete form.

The Reiki Master will usually ask everyone to meet again at the end of this period so they can share their experiences and he or she can answer questions. After-support is important. Ideally there will be a local Reiki sharing group, usually run by a Reiki Master, so that people can meet up to give group treatments and discuss experiences. If there isn't one, discuss with your Reiki Master the best way in which your practice of Reiki can be supported before you consider going on to take the Second Degree (see page 56).

Right: This simple position is taken from the full body treatment (see page 85) and is something which can be practised after First Degree initiation. Place your palms over the eyes and cheeks of the recipient and hold the position for three minutes.

second degree reiki

The decision to take the Second Degree in Reiki ideally reflects a commitment on the part of the student to become both more deeply involved with Reiki and with their own life. Taking the Second Degree is not an automatic next step and individuals should consider it carefully. It means becoming more involved with your own life because the processes that the attunement takes you through are deeply connected to your mental and emotional being. In the First Degree class (see page 54) the changes caused by receiving the attunements are primarily felt in the physical body, and most of the 'clearing out' that happens afterwards is connected with the physical body along with personal habits or patterns of behaviour that affect it. In the Second Degree the student is confronted by the mental and emotional patterns that can negatively affect their progress through life.

The minimum period of time between taking the First Degree and the Second is generally agreed to be three months by the traditional Usui school. There are two main reasons for having a minimum period between the two classes. The first is to allow the student time to adjust to the new energy in their body and to reflect on and appreciate the changes. The second is to allow them time to understand fully how Reiki

works. Rushing into the Second Degree can mean that the student doesn't have time to become familiar with the basic energy of Reiki. However, the interval between taking the Degrees is a matter of individual choice, and while some may prefer to wait months or years, others may decide to wait only a few days.

In the Second Degree class the student receives only one attunement. This further opens the chakras and allows the student to use the three symbols that amplify the Reiki energy and facilitate distance healing (see page 38). Learning and working with symbols is the key aspect of the Second Degree, as the hand positions for treating the self and others have all been learnt in the First Degree, with the exception of one new position that is specifically for mental and emotional healing. This position is the fourth position on the head (see page 72).

There is currently much controversy over the Reiki symbols. The teaching of the traditional Usui school is that the symbols are sacred and must be kept secret. In the Second Degree class the student is first taught how to draw the symbols and sign them in the air. Any paper that they have been drawn on is usually ceremonially burnt at the end of the class and the student is asked not to reveal them to anyone. The student is expected to memorize them completely by the end of the class, although I have never heard anyone say that they were not permitted to draw them for themselves at home. The symbols have been published in a number of books and can be found on the Internet, causing uproar amongst

the traditionalists. Those authors who have decided to publish them give, I think, reasons for their actions that are rational and have integrity. It is for each person to decide whether it is right or wrong for the symbols to be published and to make their judgement based on their own understanding.

Once the symbols have been learnt the student will be taught how to send distance healing to others. The Master usually asks each person to bring along photos of themselves at a younger age and other members of their family. Using the distance healing technique, Reiki is sent to each person's past and to family members. Working with the photos in this way usually continues for 21 days after the class and it is advisable to keep a journal of the experiences and emotions that this work brings up. Both my parents are dead, and I found that this aspect of Second Degree revealed things to me about their lives that helped me to understand them better and to feel compassion where before I had felt anger. It is also a very profound experience to send Reiki to your childhood. I found that to re-experience it, as I did whenever I sent Reiki to my past, allowed me to release many negative things that I could now see affecting me in the present.

Right: Learning to work with the Reiki symbols is an important aspect of Second Degree initiation. The symbols are used in the full body treatment (see page 88) and are drawn lightly in the centre of the forehead, over the recipient's Sixth *Chakra*.

third degree reiki

The Third Degree trains the student to become a Reiki Master and teacher. Here the thinking of the traditional and the independent schools differs quite radically, and again it is an issue of some contention between them. Within the traditional school only a few students are permitted to train to become Reiki Masters. This does not necessarily mean that the approach is elitist. Instead, it is based on the idea that in order to become a Reiki Master the student must have a certain depth of understanding of Reiki and a high level of commitment to it. They must also have reached the point where they are able to take full responsibility for their own lives and have a mature understanding of the processes involved in achieving that, as they will be teaching others who are about to go through the same process. It is extremely difficult to teach others if you have not yet learnt all the lessons yourself.

Within the traditional school, students who are considering training to become a Reiki Master will generally be expected to have been practising Reiki for some time. There is no definite length and the Master who is approached to give the training will evaluate each student individually. They will accept the student for training if they think they are ready and, importantly, if they are convinced that this is the right step for the student to take.

Traditional Masters rarely train more than two people at a time and in most cases it is only one. The training usually takes one year before the final attunement is given. During this period the student will assist the Master at First and Second Degree classes (see pages 54 and 56). They will also perform a number of services for the Master, such as organizing sharing groups and doing administrative work for the classes. It is very similar to an apprenticeship and the Master will teach them advanced practices of Reiki throughout the training period along with the more practical teaching approaches.

If you are considering taking this step you should approach a Reiki Master and discuss it with them carefully. They will probably ask you to write to them setting out your reasons for wanting to become a Reiki Master. Within the Usui tradition Mrs Takata set the cost of becoming a Reiki Master at $10,000 or the equivalent. This is not a small sum for most people and it is meant to reflect the commitment necessary to undertake the training. In Eastern cultures students of a spiritual path must commit years of their lives to studying with a teacher before they are considered ready to teach others. In the West we do not have the time to make that kind of commitment, nor do we have it as a tradition, so it would be difficult for most of us to envisage it. Therefore, at its most simplistic, the $10,000 is in lieu of time.

The independent Reiki Masters take a different approach. First, they are not so stringent in their selection of students; second, training may only take two days to a week; and third, the cost is significantly lower. The reason most often given for this is that the Usui tradition, with its highly priced training, effectively excludes a large number of people who would be excellent Masters and teachers. It is also argued that more healers are needed in the world and that this is not the time for exclusivity.

These arguments, particularly the first, cannot be dismissed out of hand. Each person must examine their own needs and beliefs and then make a decision. For example, some people believe that if becoming a Reiki Master is their destiny $10,000 will somehow appear at the right time. Others, however, feel that this kind of belief encourages spiritual egotism. Essentially, becoming a Reiki Master is about wanting to assist others in realizing their full human and spiritual potential and doing it without ego. This is a main consideration when deciding if becoming a Master is the right step and when choosing a Master to train you.

Right: The Reiki symbols can be used as part of a self-healing routine. By signing them over the body you can amplify the energy drawn there.

choosing a reiki master

In most cases people make their choice of a Reiki Master based on the recommendation of friends. This is a fairly reliable way of doing it, although it must be remembered that the needs and beliefs of friends are not the same as your own. Some people also like to use runes or tarot cards for guidance. Many people find their Reiki Master through some synchronicity that leads them to the right person at the right time. As with other spiritual paths, the Reiki student will experience this type of 'coincidence' repeatedly.

My own experience of finding both Reiki and a Reiki Master had an element of synchronicity. One day a close friend lent me a book that her sister had sent from India. It was by Paula Horan and was entitled *Empowerment through Reiki*. As I was off work with flu that day I had time to read it. I knew then that I wanted to practise Reiki but my friend didn't know of anyone teaching it in the UK at that time. I felt sure that I would find a teacher in the UK, and a couple of weeks later as I was walking home I passed a chemist's shop that also sold natural remedies and wholefoods. Displayed in the window was a magazine called *Kindred Spirit*, and I bought a copy. In it were pages of advertisements placed by therapists, including a Reiki Master who lived a short distance from me. I immediately made an appointment for

a treatment and had my first experience of Reiki, an experience that reinforced my desire to become a practitioner. I did not take this Master's class because she had certain beliefs that I did not feel comfortable with, so I searched for another teacher by looking up a directory of 'alternative' organizations in a bookshop where I found a listing for a Reiki organization. I telephoned the number given, and although the organization no longer existed, the woman I spoke to gave me the names of two Reiki Masters in the London area. I contacted one, and following a long conversation with her I decided to take her next First Degree class (see page 54).

Feeling at ease

It is important to examine the differences of approach to the teaching of Reiki before embarking on study. This can be done by reading books by people from both traditions and by talking to the Masters themselves. Many Masters also offer introductory lectures that can assist in making the decision. It is also vital to talk to the Master before taking their class. Using your inner guidance you should feel a strong degree of compatibility with them, combined with a feeling of trust and respect. If you don't have the sense that they are somebody you want to make a journey with or you feel that you will not be completely safe with them, then look for another one.

The reason it is essential for you to trust the Master is that you will be opening up parts of yourself that may have been hidden for years. If you feel unable to communicate these emotions safely within the group, part of the purpose of taking the class is lost. Masters who only work with small groups are usually more able to create a 'safe space' to work in, so it is advisable to check the size of the class with them. If you have never done work in groups where emotions are released, it might be worth mentioning this and discussing any fears you have about that. Most of us are uncomfortable about crying in front of other people and are also uncomfortable with other people's tears. This type of emotional release doesn't always happen in a class, but it is important that when it does the Master knows how to handle it within the group.

If you take the First Degree with one Master and feel that this was not the right person for you, then you should look for another one to teach you the Second Degree, if you decide to do it.

the universal use of symbols

The Reiki symbols, taught during the Second Degree and in the Master's training (see pages 56 and 58) are an important aspect of Reiki, and differentiate it from other healing methods in that they introduce the esoteric and occult. By using the term occult, I mean it in its correct sense – revealing that which is hidden. The Reiki symbols help us to reveal aspects of ourselves that are hidden within us. We then come to know these and, in doing so, transform ourselves. These symbols also reveal aspects of the universe beyond the material world. In the world of scientific materialism, distance or absent healing (see page 38) is judged to be impossible, but if one believes that it is possible to operate in a universe outside our conception of space and time then distance healing makes sense. Use of the Reiki symbols allows us to work in that other universe and at the same time activates the Reiki energy in specific ways.

One question must be as to why Reiki uses symbols when other forms of healing do not. The answer to this lies partly in the fact that Reiki is a spiritual path as well as a method of healing, and partly in the nature of all symbols.

Symbols have been used in all cultures since the earliest times. They possess a power that words can never have, containing as they do a multitude of meanings that speak to the intellect, to the emotion and to the soul. Many of the symbols that still hold the most power for us today have their origins in ancient cultures, when they were widely used in art and religious ritual. Alongside the visual symbols are those symbols that appear in all mythology and fairy stories and there is also the symbolism of our dreams. Often we cannot express what a particular symbol means, but we know that it speaks to us and it is something we feel in our hearts rather than our minds. Symbols challenge us to go beyond the obvious and often the simplest have the most complex meanings.

That symbols have great power cannot be denied. One only has to consider Hitler's misuse of the Hindu swastika. It is doubtful that most Westerners could look at a swastika without being overwhelmed by the negative connotations of its association with Nazism. Yet to a Hindu it is a beautiful symbol of light and of male and female energy. The advertising industry also relies heavily on the power of the symbol, using traditional ones to appeal to our emotions while trying to create new ones that will elicit the same type of emotional response – the Nike swoosh being one example.

Some symbols appear to be culturally specific, but, as with many religious beliefs, if we look at the broad canvas we will find that a symbol that is predominantly associated with one culture also appears in others, albeit in a slightly different form. The cross is one example of this.

The cross is predominantly associated with Christianity, and due to the spread of Christianity around the globe it is probably one of the most universally potent symbols. For Christians the cross is the symbol of God's forgiveness and His promise of eternal life. It also signifies the union of the divine with the human or the union of heaven and earth – the vertical representing the divine/heaven and the horizontal the human/earth. That is a very basic interpretation of the significance of the Christian cross, and if one contemplates it further, as with all symbols the layers of meaning will start to peel away until it reveals a uniquely personal meaning.

There are of course other crosses. There is the Celtic cross, a shape that brings together the cross and the circle. Its origins are in the older earth religions – the cross represents male procreative energy and the circle the female counterpart. There is also the Egyptian ankh, which again predates the Christian cross. This ancient symbol represents the key to unlocking the mysteries of heaven and earth and is also a symbol of immortality. It also combines the symbol of Osiris/male energy – the T cross – and the symbol of Isis/female energy in the oval top. Thus there are common threads connecting the crosses – the balance of

Right: The cross is predominantly recognised throughout the world as a symbol of Christianity. However, the Celtic cross has pagan origins which unite the cross and the circle as representative of male and female fertility. This Celtic cross is taken from the Lindisfarne Gospels (c. 698 AD).

male/female energy, the union of heaven and earth and the concept of immortality.

Another symbol that turns up across cultures and that is of particular interest to Reiki practitioners is the spiral. Spirals and endless knots are particularly evident in Celtic decoration, with the spiral signifying the movement of energy and the endless knot representing eternity. In the yoga tradition the kundalini energy that can lead to ultimate enlightenment is at the base of the spine and is usually represented symbolically by a coiled serpent. This is effectively a spiral shape. It is also believed that all energy flows in spirals and that this represents the solar and lunar, male and female energies. Another belief is that clockwise spirals bring energy in, while anticlockwise spirals can be used to disperse negative energy. This ancient concept of the spiral as representing the life force is reinforced by the discovery that the shape of human DNA is also a spiral.

Yet another symbol of power is the pentagram or pentacle. This endless five-pointed star has the qualities of the circle and signifies wholeness. Its points symbolize the elements of fire, air, earth and water and the spirit, and it is used in ceremonial magic to banish negative energy. Another important star-shaped symbol is the six-pointed Seal of Solomon. Like the pentagram this symbol has strong associations with magic, and through its connection with the

mystical schools of Judaism it is also represented as the Star of David. In this symbol the downward-pointing triangle represents the element of water and the feminine, while the upward-pointing triangle represents the element of fire and the masculine. The base of each triangle also bisects the apex of the other to represent the elements of air and earth. The perfect geometry of this symbol represents the balance of all these elements. It is also said that the seventh point of the triangle, being invisible, represents the spiritual element, and that when the symbol is meditated upon this becomes visible to the inner eye.

Mandalas and yantras are also geometric shapes that are used for meditation. These beautiful and intricate works of art depict the universe and the energy of creation. The student meditates on the image, moving their focus mentally from the outer edge to the centre until they become aware of the image's deeper meanings. The majority of mandalas contain lettering or human forms as Buddhas or other deities, whereas yantras are usually composed entirely of geometrical shapes.

Geometric shapes, such as the circle, square and triangle, have a strong effect on our emotions. Angular shapes make many people feel uncomfortable and anxious, while roundness makes them feel more relaxed. Symmetry and asymmetry in objects and shapes evoke similar reactions. The power of geometry, often referred to as sacred geometry, is becoming a popular subject of study, and it can be seen most clearly in great architecture, where particular proportions and shapes can instil feelings of calm or a connection with the spirit.

Finally, there is the symbolism of the human form. In the Judaeo-Christian tradition, God made man in His own image, and in other religions deities are often given a physical form. Therefore the human form as symbol reflects and contains the entire universe, making it perhaps the most complete object to meditate on.

The Reiki symbols can also be used as a focus of meditation. Although meditating on the symbols is not usually taught as a part of the Second Degree (see page 56), the student will gain greater understanding of the qualities of each symbol and the way in which they work by simply looking at them closely and allowing the unconscious to reveal their deeper meaning.

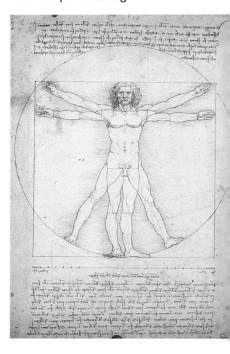

Above: Da Vinci's famous 'Vitruvian Man' is a study of human proportion. It illustrates the symbolism of the human form echoing traditional images of Christ.
Right: Mandalas depict the universe and the structure of creation. This Tibetan mandala shows Buddha at the centre of an intricate geometric design.

self-treatment

It is widely acknowledged in both Eastern and Western healing systems from acupuncture to psychoanalysis that the healer or therapist must achieve a balance within their own Mind, Body and Spirit before they are ready to help others.

Self-treatment is central to the practice of Reiki – the first person Dr Usui gave Reiki to was himself. Following the First Degree initiation (see page 54) you are asked to give yourself a full self-treatment daily for 21 days – 21 representing the number of days Dr Usui meditated for on Mount Kuri Yama before he received the Reiki symbols. It also takes three days for the new energy to move through each of the seven main *chakras* and adjust their vibratory rate. This 21-day cleansing period is just the beginning of a lifetime of self-treatment. If you are unable to manage a full self-treatment every day, try it for 10–15 minutes, for instance before you go to sleep at night or when you wake up in the morning.

Reiki is a gift to yourself and self-treatment is an acknowledgment that you are willing to take responsibility for your own life.

'The practice of Reiki is that of sharing and caring. Caring for oneself is a necessary precursor to effective caring for others. The exhortation "Physician, heal thyself!" is especially relevant to all who would practise the subtle art of Reiki. To care for yourself with Reiki allows for an expansion beyond the limits of yesterday to a blossoming of unrealized and unexpected potential for tomorrow.'

Reiki Master **Don Alexander**

self-treatment positions

Regardless of whether you choose to sit or lie down to give a self-treatment, you should always make sure that you are comfortable. Try to ensure that there are as few distractions as possible – put the answering machine on or even unplug the phone. Some people like to give themselves a treatment while they soak in the bath. My favourite time is on weekend mornings before I get up and before I go to sleep at night. If you give yourself a treatment before you go to sleep you may find that you drop off before you get through all of the positions. Don't worry if that happens – at least you will sleep well.

There are set positions for the self-treatment, so when you give yourself a full treatment you should follow the order shown here. However, if you only have a few minutes to give yourself Reiki, perhaps while travelling or watching television, you may prefer to concentrate on just one area of your body, such as the throat, stomach or kidneys. My favourite position when I feel tired or particularly if I feel upset or off-balance is to place my hands on the Fourth *Chakra* and on the Second *Chakra* (see page 75). This is also the position I use when I am preparing myself to give a Reiki treatment to another person. Let your intuition guide you to where you most need Reiki at that moment and you will feel the

benefit, even if you have not given yourself a full self-treatment.

For example, on one occasion while trying to work, I found that I didn't have the energy to do anything. Rather than trying to carry on I decided to lie down for 15 minutes and give myself some Reiki. I had been having a discussion about the kidneys some days before in relation to Chinese medicine, and as this came into my mind, I thought it best to give Reiki to my kidneys. When I placed my hands on them I found that they were indeed very cold, indicating that there was an energy block there. I gave myself Reiki until the cold feeling went – not much longer than 15 minutes. The difference in the way I felt was remarkable – I was full of energy, I could think more clearly and I was able to complete the work I was doing with ease.

The following self-treatments are, with two exceptions, taught by the traditional Usui school. You can vary them according to your needs, although you should give yourself a full treatment as often as possible.

When people start giving Reiki treatments they often worry about holding the positions for the right amount of time, and without being able to see a clock, as with Position 1, they feel that they are unable to estimate it. Don't become overly concerned about holding the positions for three minutes, just hold the position for what you feel is the right amount of time.

In some books on Reiki there is frequent mention of the hands instantly becoming hot as the energy begins to flow. This is not necessarily the case. If, when you put your hands on your

face, your hands don't feel hot or tingly, rest assured that the energy is still being channelled through your hands. Also, don't think that just because your hands aren't hot you are 'not doing it properly'.

When I start a self-treatment I sometimes find that my hands go colder rather than hotter and that my forehead is cold. However, after a few minutes my hands warm up and I can feel the energy flowing through to remove any blocks. Once I feel that enough energy has been taken into the area, I move onto the next position. After some time you will recognize a pattern in the flow of the energy. I would personally describe its movement as starting slowly, then moving faster and then slowing again as each body area recieves the optimum amount of energy it needs.

Position 1

Place your hands over your face with your palms over your eyes and the upper part of your cheeks (see left). Your fingertips should be just above your hairline, and your fingers and thumbs should be kept close together. Hold the position for at least three minutes.

Position 2

This position is a good one to use on its own if you have earache or if you are having problems with your teeth. Cup your hands over your ears, still keeping your fingers together. Hold the position until you feel ready to move on. If you have toothache, you can also cup your hands over your jaw.

Position 3

Although this position can be done quite easily sitting up, as seen here, it is easier to do when lying down as there is less strain on the arms.

Move your hands to the back of your head and cup your head in your hands (see above and left). Your thumbs should meet and touch in the middle and the base of your palms should rest just under the bone at the base of your skull.

Position 4

This position can only be done by those with Second Degree Reiki as it involves using two of the symbols (see page 56).

Keep your left hand on the back of your head in a position that is comfortable for you and doesn't involve you twisting your wrist around. Using your right hand, draw the symbols on the centre of your forehead and then place this hand across your forehead, covering it completely (see left and right).

Positions 5a and 5b

There are two positions for treating the throat area. Use whichever you find most comfortable, and again hold the position until you are ready to move on to the main body positions.

5a Keeping your fingers together, place your left hand around the back of your neck. Then loosely cup your right hand around the front of your throat area, with your thumb pointing towards your right ear. You can reverse this and put your right hand on the back of your neck if you wish (see above).

5b Or, as shown here (above left), hold this position by cupping both of your hands together in front of your neck with your fingertips going just behind and under your ears.

Positions 6a and 6b

These two positions treat the stomach, the spleen and the liver and are useful on their own if your stomach is feeling upset or if you feel the spleen and liver need some help in getting rid of body toxins.

6a For the first body position (see above) place your hands across the solar plexus area, palms down and fingertips touching in the middle. Remember to keep your fingers together.

6b When you have finished giving Reiki here, move your hands down, though keeping them in the same position, so that your middle fingers are just above your navel and give Reiki to this area.

Position 7

This position treats the pelvic area and the reproductive organs. It is a good position for women to use when their period is starting as it will help to relieve any cramping pain.

Place the heels of your palms on each of your hip bones and point your fingers down and into the middle so that your fingertips touch (see below). You can keep your thumbs in close to your hands or spread them outwards, making a heart shape between your hands.

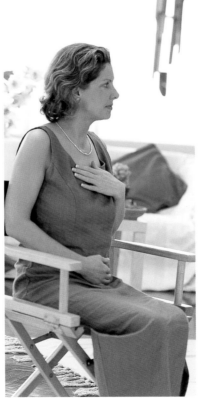

Position 8

The last of the front body positions is one that helps to balance the energy. This is the position that I use before starting to give a Reiki treatment to another person. When you are holding this position you are connecting your heart energy with the centre that stores energy or *Chi* in the body (see page 18). This centre is called the *hara* in the Indian yoga tradition and the *Tan T'ien* in Chinese medicine and Qigong.

Place one hand over the Second *Chakra* area, just below the navel, and the other over the Fourth *Chakra*, which is beside the physical heart in the centre of the breastbone area (see above and left).

Positions 9a and 9b

Clearly there is no way that you can comfortably treat the whole of your back by yourself. Instead, self-treatment on the back focuses on the kidneys and the adrenals just above the kidneys (see page 22).

9a and 9b For both of these positions, place the palms of your hands on each side of your back with your fingers pointing into your spine (see above). If your back is not very broad your fingertips will touch. To cover the adrenals, place the outside edge of your hands slightly over the bottom of the ribcage and your hands will naturally be in place.

Position 10

The shoulders are the only other back areas that are reasonably accessible, and as we store so much tension in them it is a good idea to give them Reiki whenever we can. This is a good position to use while you take a break from working on a computer or while you are watching television.

The position can be done in two ways. Cross your arms in front of you and place your hands on the back of each shoulder (see above and right).

Alternatively, instead of crossing your arms in front of you, put your right hand over the back of your right shoulder and your left hand behind your left shoulder and point your fingers towards your spine.

Positions 11 and 12

These positions are additional and are not taught by the traditional Usui Masters as part of a self-treatment. They can easily be done in the bath or as part of giving yourself a foot massage or reflexology treatment (see page 28).

11 The first is giving Reiki to your knees. The knees can hold stagnant energy and fear, as well as being problem areas for people with arthritis and rheumatism. I have included them in the full self-treatment, but they can be done separately. Place your hands on your knees and hold the position for three minutes (see below).

12 Similarly, your feet and ankles, which do so much hard work, can be treated by simply placing your hands around them in a way that is comfortable for you (see above and right).

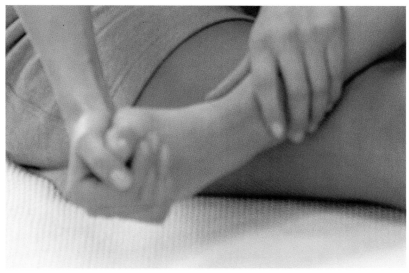

treating others

Reiki is a simple, non-intrusive and powerful method of treating others. It is simple because it requires no elaborate or difficult techniques. It is non-intrusive because it does not require the recipient to remove their clothes and because there is no pressure applied to the body. This makes it particularly useful for treating conditions where touching the body may be painful as in the case of someone who has been burnt or is recovering from surgery. And it is powerful because the Reiki energy goes to the deeper levels of the recipient's being, where many illnesses originate. Also, a Reiki treatment will complement and increase the effectiveness of most kinds of medication and other forms of treatment.

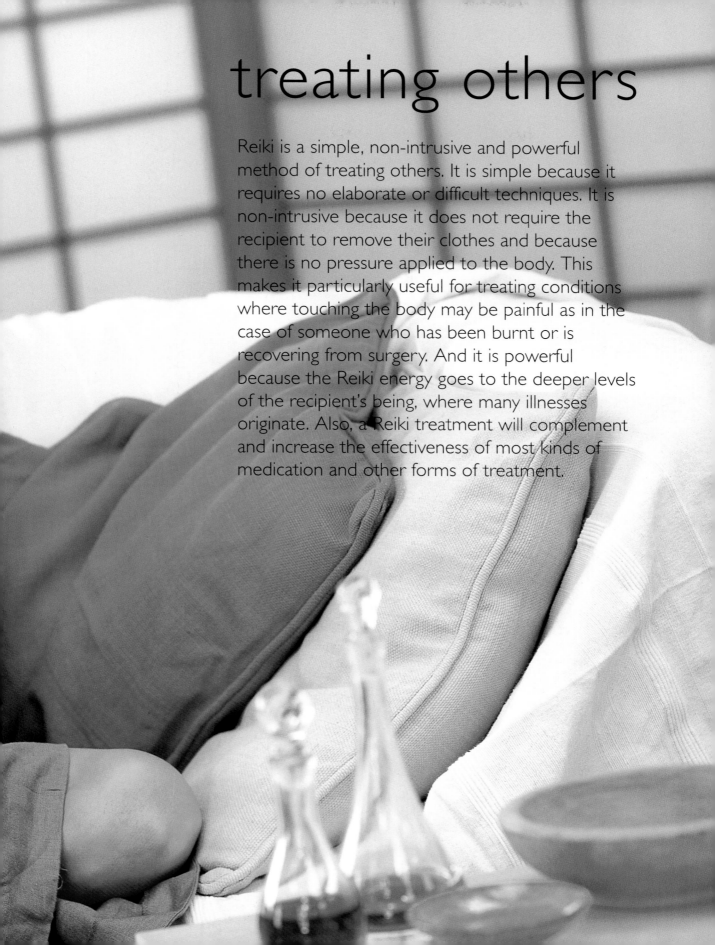

'Are you a newcomer to Reiki? Do you doubt your own ability to heal or the ability of Reiki to work for you? I would urge you to follow the simple advice of umpteen business and self-help gurus and "just do it!" – that is the key. Whether you give 10 treatments, 100 treatments or 1000 treatments, Reiki will teach you all you need to learn. You will build a field of gratitude and an aura of grace around yourself that will be your joy and the joy of others in your life.'

Reiki Master **Don Alexander**

positions for treating others

Although an important, and perhaps primary, use of Reiki is for healing the self, once you have received the initial attunements there is a responsibility and desire to use Reiki for healing others. There are different ways to approach this: some people prefer to keep it informal, treating only family and friends, while others want to set up a business as a Reiki practitioner, working from home or from a clinic offering complementary therapies. Either way brings up another Reiki issue – that of charging for treatments.

It is said that Dr Usui's experience in the Beggars' Quarter made him realize that when Reiki was given freely, the receiver felt no need to take responsibility for their own life. This part of the Reiki story is used by many teachers to illustrate why when someone receives a Reiki treatment there should be an exchange of energy. The 'energy' that the recipient exchanges for the treatment is most often money, but it may be a service. When you are treating family members there is no need to consider the issue, as energy is exchanged between all of the people in the family, all of the time. This is often the case with friends as well. However, if you hope to earn all or most of your living from practising Reiki, you will have to charge a fee for your services. One way to establish what you will

charge is to ask the people in your local Reiki group. Also, you will probably have received a treatment at some time – how did you feel about the amount you paid? Therapists working from clinics often charge more than those working from home because they have more business overheads; likewise those for whom Reiki is the sole source of income will probably charge slightly more as well. If you think the charges for Reiki are too high, fix a price that you feel comfortable with. If you can afford to make reductions for people who are on a low income or unemployed, then do it. It is rather meaningless to talk about healing the world and healing other people if this is limited to those who can afford it, and in the West complementary therapies are not cheap. Those who cannot afford to pay with money may be able to offer you something else – gardening, baby-sitting or house repairs, for example. Whatever way you choose, the important thing is that you and the recipient feel comfortable.

Before you begin the treatment, you will have prepared yourself and your treatment room (see pages 32–5). If this is the recipient's first treatment you will need to allow extra time before the session for talking to them about their reasons for coming and any medical problems they may have. A Reiki treatment usually lasts an hour, with each position taking 3–5 minutes, but if the recipient has a lot to discuss, allow an extra 30 minutes. Some practitioners stick strictly to an hour, but I feel this does not leave much time for the recipient to discuss their experience of the treatment. If I don't have time to

talk to them afterwards, I may tell them that they can phone me if they are having any unusual experiences or worries about the treatment.

The first five positions of a treatment are on the head and throat areas. With these positions you will treat the Fifth, Sixth and Seventh *Chakras* and the pineal, pituitary and thyroid glands. When moving between positions, try to ensure that you make no sudden movements – your hands should flow from one position to the next. Practice, self-confidence and steady breathing should help you to achieve this. Also, try to maintain hand contact with the recipient throughout, because if you move away from the table they may feel vulnerable. After giving a few treatments you will find there is a natural flow and all your movements will be in harmony with that flow.

Positions 1a, 1b and 1c

1a Have the recipient lie comfortably on her back on the treatment table, hands by her sides, not folded over her stomach, and seat yourself behind her head. As a starting position, rest your hands gently on the recipient's shoulders for a few moments (see top left). This helps you to tune into her energy flow.

1b Place your hands together, with the sides of your thumbs touching and your palms facing downwards, a few centimetres/inches above the recipient's face. Slowly lower your hands onto her face, ensuring that your thumbs are placed in the middle of her forehead and slightly over the top of the bridge of her nose (see top right).

1c Then place your palms over her eyes and lightly rest your fingers on her cheeks. Hold the position for three minutes (see above left).

Positions 2a and 2b

There are variations on some of the positions depending on the preference of the Master. Shown here are two variations on the second position, both of which were taught to me by Masters of the traditional school. The first position is Mrs Takata's; the second is a commonly found variation.

2a Place the palms of your hands over each of the recipient's ears, with your thumbs in front of her ears. Your fingers should fall into a natural position over the back of her jaw and neck (see above).

2b Place the heel of your palm above each temple with your palms over the temples. Your fingers should lie against the side of her face, with the little fingers resting in front of each ear (see left).

Positions 3a, 3b, 3c and 3d

It takes some practice to manoeuvre your hands gracefully into these positions. Breathe into your centre and don't rush it! Many recipients feel tense when you are manoeuvring them into this position and are unable to allow you to fully support their head and neck. Encourage them to let you take the weight of their head, but don't mention it too many times or they will just become more self-conscious. Relaxed or not, this is a favourite position for many people. I think this is because it echoes the way a mother holds a baby's head. After a treatment, some people have singled out this position as the one that makes them feel 'very cared for'.

3a Slide your right hand from over the recipient's ear (see 2a) onto the side of her cheek (see top left).

3b Next, place your left hand on the left side of the recipient's face and slowly push her head over to the right, so that the back of your right hand is now touching the table (see left).

3c Now place your left hand under the back of her head with the fingers pointing down and over part of her neck (see below left).

3d Slowly roll the recipient's head over to the left so that the back of your left hand is touching the table and her head is supported in your left palm. Bring your right hand in under the back of her head so that your hands are cradling her head and the top of her neck. Make sure your hands are comfortable and that her head feels secure and balanced (see below).

Positions 4a and 4b

This position entails using the symbols for mental healing as taught in the Second Degree (see page 56). These are drawn over the centre of the forehead. With both hands under the head in the previous position, choose which hand you will use to draw the symbols.

4a Slide that hand down the back of the recipient's neck to support it while you move your other hand into the centre back of her head. Adjust your hand until you are satisfied that you can take the full weight of her head. Remember, you are not holding her head up – the back of your hand should be flat on the table. Now slide your other hand out from under her neck and draw the symbols over her forehead with your index finger (see right).

4b Then place your closed fingers over her forehead, fingers pointing downwards, and the rest of your hand over the top of her head (see left). After holding this position for 3–5 minutes, first remove your hand from her forehead and slip it back under her neck. This provides support while you slowly slide your other hand out from under her head, pulling your hand towards you. The recipient may again lift her head to help you with this movement; quietly tell her to relax and let you do the work.

Positions 5a and 5b

Some people find it uncomfortable to have another person's hands too close to their throat and you should consider this when deciding how to treat this area. Also, the throat is an area that holds an enormous amount of emotional issues for many people and during treatment some very strong images, emotions and even physical pain can surface.

5a First rest your elbows on either side of the recipient's head (but not too close) and bring your hands in front of her throat area, approximately 7.5 cm/3 inches away from her throat. Interlace your fingers with the tips of your thumbs just touching (it doesn't matter if they don't) and cup her jawline and throat area (see right).

There are variations on this position. Simply lay your hands on each side of the recipient's jaw with your thumbs just above her jawbone and your fingers pointing towards each other, but not interlaced. This version brings your hands closer to her throat area, while in the position shown, your hands should be kept some distance from her throat.

5b Finish by unlacing your fingers and pulling your arms away in an arc until they reach the edge of the table (see below).

Position 6

Having finished the recipient's head and throat area you then move on to treat the rest of the front of her body. To do these positions you will need to stand up unless you have the type of office chair that moves around on castors.

For the first body position, place your hands, one behind the other, beneath the chest area (on women, just below the breasts), across the ribs (see right). Hold the position for three minutes.

Positions 7a and 7b

7a To move from the previous position into this one, you can either keep your hands in the same position and just slide them down the recipient's body 2.5–5cm/1–2 inches, or you can use a technique employed by massage therapists, where you slide the hand farthest from you towards you and down the body, while sliding the hand nearest to you across to the other side (see right). You can use this crisscross motion for the body positions on the back as well as the front of the body.

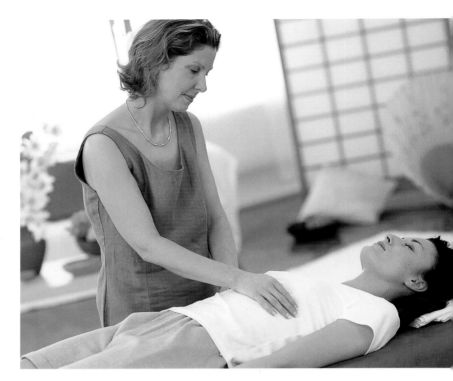

7b An alternative way to do the sixth and seventh positions is to start by placing your hands together on one side of the recipient's body, holding the position for three minutes, then slide both of your hands over to the other side of her body (see left). What is important with both methods is that you cover the *chakras* and the major organs.

Position 8

This position treats the pelvic area.

Place your left hand on the inner side of the recipient's right hip bone, fingers together and pointing down towards her pubic bone. Then place the heel of your right hand a small distance from your left fingertips, pointing your hand upwards on the inner side of her left hip bone so that your hands are making a V-shape (see left).

Position 9

This position concludes treating the front of the body by balancing and linking the energy in the upper and lower body.

Place your right hand on the recipient's abdomen and your left hand on her breastbone, fingers pointing to her head (see below).

11 Then stand at the bottom of the table and move your hands down to the ankles and feet, holding them with your hands pointing upwards (see below).

Next ask the recipient to turn over onto her stomach. As most recipients are very relaxed by now, tell her to turn over slowly. You can arrange her hands by her sides, although some people prefer to rest their head on their arms. This is fine but it does make it more difficult for you to do the first back position, as their muscles are scrunched up. One solution is to ask them to keep their arms by their sides just while you do the first position.

Positions 10 and 11

These positions are additional and are not taught by Mrs Takata. Use these positions if you feel they are appropriate to the needs of the recipient, or use them to find out the sequence of treatment positions that you think works best for most recipients.

10 The first position treats the knees (see above). You move from the pelvic position to this position, one hand at a time. Hold the position for three minutes.

Position 12

The shoulders hold a lot of tension for most people. Some recipients' shoulders feel like sponges soaking up energy and you may find that your hands don't want to leave this position. This feeling of your hands being glued into a position can occur at any time during a Reiki treatment, so it is best just to stay in the position until your hands feel ready to move, as that area of the body obviously needs extra energy.

Lay your hands across the recipient's shoulders, in the same way as on the front of her body. I find it slightly easier on my hands and arms if I do not keep my hands in a straight line, but instead allow them to curve a little so that one hand is pointing slightly upwards and the other downwards (see below).

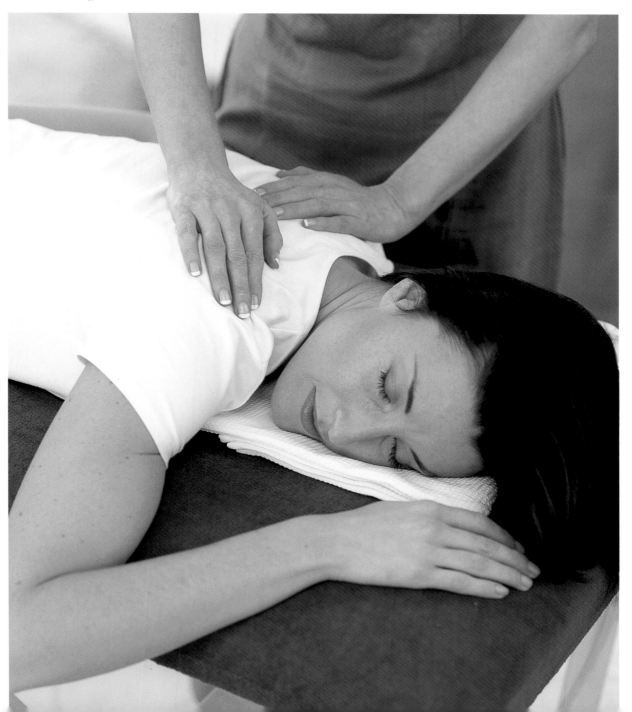

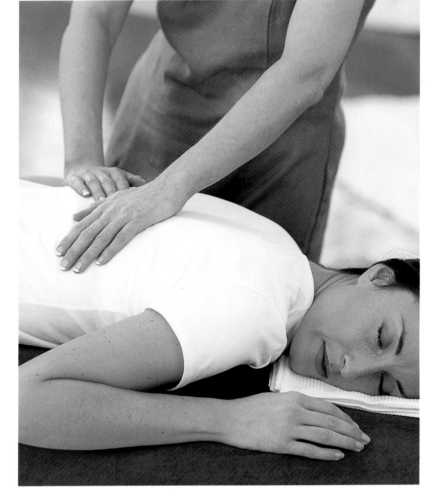

Position 13

Move your hands from her shoulders down to the back of the heart area and hold for three minutes (see left). If you have time, you can cover the area just below this as well before moving on to the adrenals and the kidneys.

Position 14

To cover the adrenals and kidneys completely you will probably need to do this position in stages. Move your hands down the recipient's back from the previous position, first covering her adrenals, and then move your hands down again and cover her kidneys (see left). If the recipient has back pain around the tail end of the spine, you may want to keep moving your hands down until you have covered the whole area. If your recipient is male you can treat the prostate gland by placing one of your hands on top of the other in the centre of his buttocks, just below the tailbone, after you have completed the back positions.

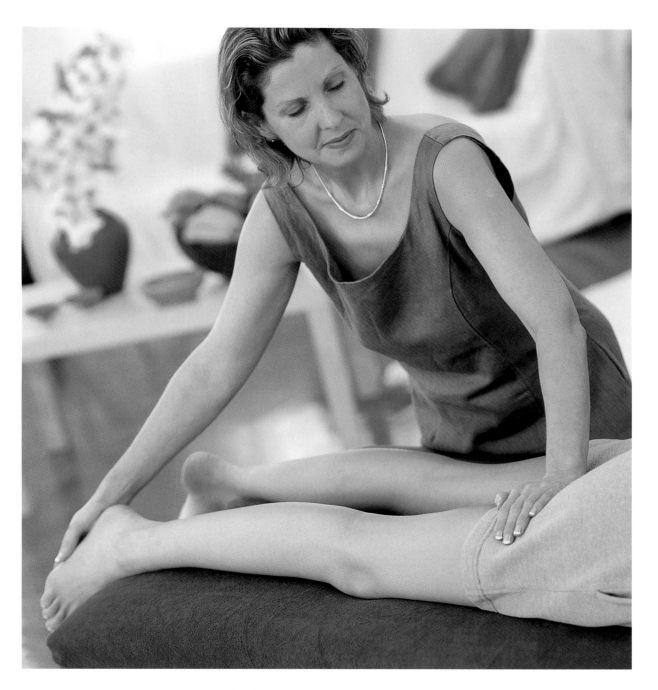

Position 15

This last position needs to be done in
two stages.

15a Place one of your hands at the top of
the recipient's leg nearest to you and place
your other hand flat against the sole of her
foot. Hold this position for three minutes.

15b Then stand at the other side of the
table to do her other leg. When I move
around the bottom of the table to get to
the other side, I hold onto one of the
recipient's feet so that contact is not lost.
You then repeat the position on the
recipient's other leg and foot. You can lean
across the table to do this position,
provided you do not find it puts strain on
your back (see above).

Clearing the aura

Now that you have finished the treatment, all that remains is to clear the aura and help the recipient to feel grounded before she gets up. There are many ways to clear the aura and I have tried several of them. Shown here is the method of the traditional school.

1a and 1b Place your hands on the sides of the recipient's hips (see above) and pull firmly down to her feet (see right). Shake off the excess energy from your hands. Do this a total of three times.

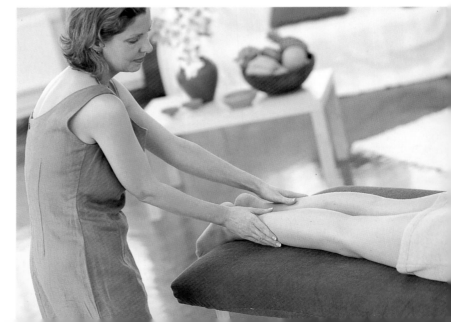

2a and 2b Then place your hands on her back, around the waist area (see above). Push your hands up towards her heart and outwards over each shoulder and down the outsides of her arms (see right). Shake off the excess energy from your hands. Do this also a total of three times.

I then leave the room quietly so that the recipient can get up in her own time. I wash my hands to finish the session symbolically and clear myself of any of the recipient's energy. You can then bring water to the recipient and discuss the treatment, but only if she wants to talk.

Finally, I don't believe in pushing people into making further appointments for treatments – I prefer to leave it open so that they can make a decision without feeling pressured.

treating children

Most children are very receptive to Reiki energy and are fascinated by the idea of it. This is not surprising when you consider the popularity of children's television programmes in which the heroic characters all have 'special powers'. Friends' children sometimes ask me if I will give them Reiki, which I happily do, although I will be lucky if the session lasts longer than three minutes, especially with the younger children. I think this is partly because they expect to be 'zapped' and they lose interest quickly when this doesn't happen.

My own child firmly resists my offers to give him Reiki. Sometimes I try to do it surreptitiously while he is sitting beside me listening to a story, but he usually says, 'I know what you're doing' and I have to stop. Consequently, I find that the easiest way to give young children Reiki is when they are sleeping. You won't be able to follow all the positions – just adapt them to the child's sleeping position so that you don't disturb them. Remember, Reiki energy will go through duvets and blankets, so you don't need to worry about only their head and shoulders being accessible. Babies and older children are easier to give Reiki to – babies because you are holding them most of the time anyway, and older children because they are able to remain still for a longer period of time.

It is also important to remember that children do not need to receive Reiki for as long as an adult. Their bodies are smaller and they have not accumulated the energy blocks that adults have. Twenty to thirty minutes should be enough for a full-body treatment, but use your judgment, and base it on the child's age, temperament and willingness to receive the energy. You can treat a child lying on a table, but if they become restless, let them sit up and talk to you while you continue giving them Reiki.

Below and right: Children are often reluctant to remain still for long periods of time. Therefore, when giving a child Reiki you should allow them to change position when they wish.

If a child is a bit apprehensive when they first arrive it is better not to rush them into starting the treatment – engage their interest in something else first. On one such occasion I got a child to help me light every candle in the room. When we got to the last one it was time to start the treatment and at this point he was happy to hop up onto the table. It was a very beautiful session as it was done completely by candlelight on a dark winter's afternoon and the child went off to sleep within minutes.

When you first give a child a full treatment, you will probably notice that the energy flows through them in a different way to an adult. Even while you are treating their head there is a feeling that the energy is going right through their body to their feet. The flow is faster because the child's energy body is more in balance with their physical body – or at least this is the case if you are treating a child who has no specific or serious problems.

If a parent asks you to treat a child who has a condition such as Down's Syndrome or cerebral palsy, you will need to consider carefully what you tell them Reiki can do for the child. You should talk to the parents about why they have chosen to bring their child to you and what they think and hope it will achieve. It would be irresponsible to offer them the hope of an outright cure, although the possibility of a miracle is always present. It is perhaps better to say that Reiki will help the child to achieve their fullest potential in a natural way.

You should also encourage parents who bring their children for treatment to receive the Reiki attunements themselves. Most children probably feel more comfortable with their own parents, and in the case of children with chronic conditions it is much more sensible for the parents to treat the child rather than take them to a Reiki practitioner every week. It also gives the parents a real sense of participating in their child's treatment. Orthodox medicine tends to exclude and patronize parents, which may result in the parents losing empathy with the child.

Children can also receive the Reiki attunements themselves. If you are practising Reiki and your child or children would like to be initiated, discuss it with your Reiki Master. They will of course have to go through the clearing out process following the attunements, but if you have already experienced it you will be able to guide them through it. Afterwards, your child or children will be able to treat you and each other, and family group treatments could become a weekly event.

Above: One of the simplest ways to
give a child Reiki is whilst they are
sleeping. However, you will need to adjust
the positions involved in a full body
treatment so as not to wake them.

group treatment

Taking part in a group treatment is a unique experience. When healing became a body-centred activity, done to an individual by another individual, we lost our understanding of the spiritual dimension of disease and the power of communal and ceremonial healing. The re-emergence of interest in the Native American sweat lodge and fire walking, to name but two examples, shows that there is a deep-seated need in all of us to

work through spiritual processes within a group ritual form.

Hopefully, your Reiki Master holds regular meetings for group treatments. If they don't and there are other Reiki practitioners in your area, you can start your own group meetings. As a group you will need to decide how long each meeting should last – as a guide, probably not longer than two hours – and how you will structure the meeting. Do you all want to begin by sharing your experiences since the last meeting and then start the treatment session, or do you want to do it the other way around? It will probably take some experimentation before you find the structure that is right for the whole group.

Also, you will need to decide who is going to lead each meeting. Ideally group members should take

it in turns. This means that everyone has responsibility and has to think about the group and the sense of ritual that they want to bring to it. It also means that everyone gets a chance to experience leading the group and their self-confidence is strengthened by doing that. Within the structure the group establishes, there should be room for each person to share their special gift. One person may want to lead the group in a visualization before the treatment begins, another may want to teach everyone a praise song or share a piece of music. Thus, healing in a group will be able to take many forms.

The method of giving a group treatment is not difficult. If the group is very large you should consider dividing yourselves into two smaller groups just for the

treatment session, otherwise you could be there for hours. If you have an hour to give the treatment and six people, then each person has 10 minutes, and you should try to keep to that. If someone comes to the meeting with a special problem, however, you may decide among yourselves to give that person extra treatment time.

In a group treatment the recipient always starts by lying on their back. The person who sits at the head of the treatment table is the one who needs to keep an eye on the time as the others must follow their movements. The other group members stand around the table and wait until the leader places their hands in the first treatment position (see page 85). They then place their hands on the part of the body nearest to them and hold that position until the leader moves to the second position (see page 86). Everyone should try to move their hands to the next position at the same time. If you are one of those standing, it is sometimes confusing as to where you should put your hands next as you will probably not be able to follow the standard body positions. The answer is, put your hands where you can find a space. If you put your hands on the recipient's knees as the first position, then you could move your hands to above the knees as your second position and so on.

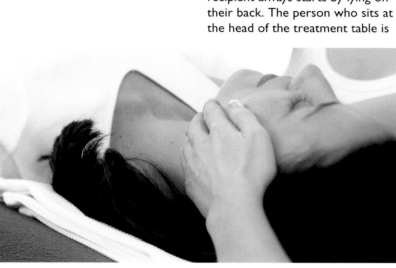

In a group treatment each position will usually be held for a shorter time so that all, or nearly all, of the head positions can be done. At the end of each member's treatment the group should finish off the treatment as they would any other, by clearing the aura (see page 96). It is also my experience of group meetings that the order in which members are treated is never decided beforehand. Instead, people get on the table when they feel it is their turn. At first I didn't think that this was a good way to do it, but the only other way I can think of is to do it by rota. This is, of course, a more organized way, but I have come to the conclusion that it does not teach us anything about ourselves within a group situation, or teach us the skill of observing the unspoken needs of others. These are as much a part of group healing as the incredible surge of energy that each person receives from the group.

remedial treatment

A practitioner cannot direct the Reiki energy to cure specific body organs or illnesses, and will in fact impede the work of the energy if they try to impose their will on it. However, a practitioner can give extra attention to diseased parts of the body. Reiki can also be used as a first-aid treatment and in certain situations, such as giving birth (see page 120).

Ideally the practitioner should focus on treating specific acute or chronic conditions after a full-body treatment has been given. This is so that the whole body, physical and energetic, can be brought into balance first. Then the practitioner can spend extra time giving Reiki to specific parts of the body. In the case of a person with breast cancer this would be the site of the tumour, or in the case of someone with a bronchial problem it would be the lungs. The exceptions to this are accidents, when the practitioner can directly treat the injury, although special precautions must be taken if the person is bleeding, or there is the possibility of broken bones. It is important to note that Reiki should never be used as a substitute for orthodox medical treatment.

'Reiki does not impose on the world a catalogue of hard and fast rules. However, in general we can say that the sooner after an accident Reiki can be given, the quicker and more complete the recovery tends to be. I have seen burns and scalds leave no mark and cuts heal in a remarkably short time. The strongest advice I can give is that you check to see whether the ailment demands any other treatment first, take whatever action is needed, then move into Reiki mode and give Reiki its chance to work.'

Reiki Master **Don Alexander**

patterns of healing

Reiki can be used for both acute and chronic conditions. An acute condition is one that is temporary, such as colds and flu, cuts and bruising, cystitis or a viral infection such as measles or chickenpox. Headaches are also acute, unless the person suffers from them on a regular basis in which case they are probably symptomatic of a chronic condition. A chronic condition is the opposite of acute and is long-term. It could also be said that an external agent, such a virus, mainly causes acute conditions, while chronic conditions are caused by an internal imbalance within the person. This is a simplistic explanation and there are of course exceptions to it.

There are some conditions that are both chronic and acute: migraine and asthma are both chronic conditions, although the actual attacks in both cases are acute. In fact many chronic conditions have acute phases where the symptoms suddenly flare up. Examples of this are eczema, psoriasis, arthritis, rheumatism and sinusitis, to name just a few. However, both orthodox and complementary medicine will usually approach all of these as chronic conditions when making a decision about treatment.

Although the Reiki practitioner cannot direct the energy to heal specific problems of either an acute or chronic nature, they need to approach acute and chronic conditions in distinct ways. Some specific acute conditions, such as burns, cuts and broken bones, are dealt with in the section on First Aid (see pages 110–15). In these examples you will find that Reiki energy can be directed to a particular spot in order to alleviate the immediate symptoms, such as bleeding, pain and shock. However, the Reiki practitioner should simply let the energy flow and not try consciously to will a particular result. You should also observe orthodox First Aid practices in such instances and combine them with Reiki.

Other acute conditions such as colds, flu and viral infections should be treated with full Reiki treatments. These should be as frequent as possible, although in many cases of acute conditions, the symptoms will disappear after one or two treatments. I used to suffer from flu regularly and found it very difficult to fully recover each time. Just before I learnt Reiki myself, I contracted flu yet again and as my friend had just become a Reiki practitioner, I asked her if she would give me a treatment. As she gave me Reiki, I felt my body become heavier and heavier until I thought that I had turned into a concrete block. Then the heaviness seemed to be flowing into the floor I was lying on. When the treatment finished, I expected to feel a little better. However, the flu had gone in that one session and I even felt better than I had before I had the flu.

In general you will probably find that acute conditions are best dealt with by a small number of full treatments (and specific spot treatments) given in quick succession. Chronic conditions, somehow reflecting themselves, need a longer-term treatment approach. The root causes of a chronic condition form at the level of mind and spirit over time before they manifest as symptoms in the physical body. This also applies to chronic conditions that manifest at or soon after the birth. If, for example, a person starts to have rheumatism in their fifties, the mental and spiritual causes of this imbalance have been forming over time through the attitudes and emotional reactions of that person.

The symptoms of disease are the methods by which we are alerted by the mind and spirit to problems at a higher level and are really a kind of stop sign that asks us to look at our lives. However, Western society has learnt to see illness as just illness, a negative thing to be overcome without any other function. As a result we find it quite difficult to get well because we are unwilling to use the time of illness to explore ourselves. Also, we are under incredible pressure from employers and others to never be sick, and so many people struggle into work while they are still unwell without pausing to contemplate why they are ill.

Once you approach illness in the light of it being a message to change, you will find that your opinion of it totally alters and you can adopt an attitude of gratitude for it. This change of attitude, when combined with Reiki treatments, will increase the speed of healing. It will also, hopefully, lead you to look at aspects of your life and character that may be the cause of the imbalance and find a way to change these. This is not something that will happen overnight, but steady work on the self, in whatever form, will show results at both the physical and mental levels.

As a Reiki practitioner, if you are treating a person with a chronic condition, you should advise them that they will in all probability need many treatments. There is no way of knowing exactly how many treatments will be required and ultimately it is their decision to continue or stop treatment. One thing that you should tell them is that when a chronic condition is treated with Reiki, it will usually get worse before it gets better. Everyone has their own healing pattern, but a common one in a chronic condition is that there is immediate relief after the first treatment. This encourages the person to return for more treatments, but then the symptoms get worse and the person becomes discouraged. This is why you must warn them beforehand of the possibility of this. You can also recommend that they use their other therapies in conjunction with the Reiki treatments and in many cases this will help to speed the process.

The important thing when you are treating people with acute or chronic conditions is to help them recognize the causes of the imbalance but in a way that does not make them self-judgmental. Encourage yourself and others to see illness as a positive gift.

first aid for common ailments and accidents

The following guidelines are for using Reiki alongside orthodox and other complementary treatments for common ailments or everyday accidents.

Acute toothache

What is it? Toothache may be a pain emanating from a tooth or several teeth. Occasionally they hurt below gum level. Most toothache is the result of tooth decay, gingivitis, sensitive teeth, inflammation of the pulp of the tooth, neuralgia, an abscess, or sinusitis (in which case the pain is referred). The pain can be a continuous throbbing or intermittent. Sometimes it is brought on by eating something that irritates the exposed nerve of the tooth. After the tooth has been treated there may be some pain but this should soon ease.

Toothache should always be investigated by a dentist but, while waiting for an appointment, there are many treatments that provide temporary symptomatic relief.

Orthodox treatment Aspirin or paracetamol will ease pain. At the surgery, the dentist will examine the mouth to identify the cause of the pain and provide treatment. Antibiotics may be prescribed for infections, for example, on the root of the nerve, in the pulp of the tooth, or where bleeding gums present the risk of one. Toothaches combined with a temperature may mean an abscess and speedy treatment is needed. An abscess may be lanced and treated by antibiotics.

Emergency treatment is needed for severe toothache that keeps a person awake at night, if the gums swell or if the side of the face where the pain is experienced becomes swollen.

Reiki treatment In the case of toothache, Reiki should be given to the whole jaw area several times a day. This is done simply by cupping the jaw in your hands, whether it is your jaw or another person's, for 10–15 minutes at a time. I also use the second head position (see page 86, 2a) when treating any tooth or gum pain, as this will also treat the throat area, which can be affected by teeth problems. When someone suffers constantly from teeth and gum problems, a series of full-body treatments are necessary as the treatments reflect a more deep-seated chronic condition.

Other therapies
Homoeopathic treatment may include coffea for toothache with severe shooting pain, chamomilla for toothache with unbearable pain and belladonna for toothache with throbbing pain, particularly if the gums and teeth are swollen. A **Western herbalist** may suggest tinctures of echinacea or myrrh to encourage healing and reduce the

Right: For acute toothache, Reiki can be given directly to the jaw area. Cup the hands gently around the recipient's jaw and hold the position for 10–15 minutes. Bursts of treatment can be repeated whilst the pain continues, although orthodox treatment from a dentist should also be sought.

risk of infection. Cayenne can act as a local anaesthetic to relieve pain. A **reflexologist** may stimulate the points on the hands and feet corresponding to the teeth. An **auricular therapist** can provide pain-relieving emergency treatment. **Bach flower** remedies' Rescue Remedy may be applied to the tooth.

Broken bones

What are they? There are several different types of fracture and the symptoms include swelling, pain, misalignment of the injured area, immobility and protrusion of bone through the skin.

Orthodox treatment Breaks and fractures are usually caused by injury and should be treated by a doctor. Watch out for shock (see page 114) and cover any bleeding with a clean cloth. Immobilize the affected joint with a sling or splint. **Do not** give any food or drink. If you suspect a neck or spine fracture **do not** move the victim. Get medical help urgently. **Do not** try to force back a dislocated joint into position yourself as this could cause more damage.

Reiki treatment If there is any suspicion that either an adult or child has broken a bone, **do not** give Reiki to the area of the break. If you do, there is a real possibility that the bone will start to knit before it has been set and then the bone will have to be re-broken. You can give Reiki to other areas of the body to help the person to relax. Get them to a hospital emergency department immediately. Once the bone has been set and the plaster cast applied, then you can give Reiki to the break area as often as you like. This will both help the bone to heal more quickly and relieve some of the skin irritation that people get from wearing a cast.

Other therapies
Western herbalists may suggest certain herbs which would help to speed the healing process, particularly comfrey. **Bach flower** remedies' Rescue Remedy can be applied to the temples and pulse points to reduce panic symptoms. An **aromatherapist** may suggest essential oils of lavender, melissa or peppermint dropped on a handkerchief and held under the nose until help arrives or the condition stabilizes. **Ayurvedic medicine** offers several treatments for emotional shock, and emergency remedies can be provided while waiting for help. After treatment for the fracture **nutritional therapists** will recommend comfrey for aiding the mending of bone breaks and fractures and zinc and vitamin C supplements. **Reflexology** will be overall; special attention will be paid to the areas of the affected part to assist formation of bone.

Burns and scalds

What are they? The difference between burns and scalds is that burns are caused by forms of dry heat, such as fire, electricity, strong sunlight or chemicals, while scalds are produced by damp heat from boiling liquids or steam.

The effects of both on the skin and soft tissues are the same, as is the treatment. With mild (first-degree) burns the damage is restricted to the outer layer of skin and symptoms include redness, soreness, heat and sometimes blistering. They can be very painful but are seldom actually dangerous unless they cover a large area. Sunburn produces first-degree burns and may also cause fever and produce some swelling of the affected skin. With more serious (second-degree) burns the damage goes deeper into the skin, damaging the lower layers and producing blisters. Third-degree burns are very serious and affect the soft tissue and nervous system deep beneath the skin. Second and third-degree burns may be accompanied by shock.

Orthodox treatment Bathe the area in cold water for 10–15 minutes and then cover it lightly with a clean bandage or cloth. **Do not** put anything else on the burn site, and certainly not butter or fat as is traditionally recommended.

Reiki treatment You can give Reiki while you are following the orthodox first aid treatment, but you should not touch the burn. For a very light burn, this may be sufficient treatment. In the case of more severe burns, you must see a doctor, although you can give Reiki as first aid to help with the initial shock and pain.

Other therapies
Aromatherapists may suggest applying a few drops of undiluted lavender oil to the site of minor burns. A **homoeopath** may recommend arnica when blistering has occurred and where there is searing, smarting pain. This should be followed by cantharis. Urticus should be taken for continuous, stinging pain. **Bach flower** remedies' Rescue Remedy can help promote healing if there is emotional stress. **Western herbalism** advises aloe vera for unbroken skin, or calendula cream on broken skin.

Right: Reiki should never be given to the area of a broken bone until after the bone has been set. However, Reiki treatments can be given to the area of the break once the plaster cast has been applied and after its removal to speed recovery.

Cuts and abrasions

What are they? Most cuts and abrasions are minor and only the capillaries are damaged, causing a small amount of blood to be released into the surrounding tissues, or to escape the wound. This blood will soon clot and requires little treatment. For severe cuts, particularly to a vein, blood loss must be stopped urgently and medical help sought.

Orthodox treatment Abrasions need to be cleaned and a loose dressing applied to keep them clean. Cuts should be cleaned and direct pressure should be applied to the bleeding area until the blood flow ceases. Holding the area upright helps achieve this. Loose dressings may be needed to keep the cut clean, although exposure to air will help healing. More severe cuts may require stitches or tissue glue to help the skin join up during healing.

Reiki treatment If a minor cut is bleeding, give Reiki to the area but without touching the open wound because you could transfer infection from your hands. Reiki will help to stop the bleeding and in some cases does so very quickly.

Other therapies
Western herbalists may suggest using calendula ointment after washing the cut with running water to remove dirt. They may also recommend soaking cotton wool in a calendula and water mix and holding it over the site of the wound. An **aromatherapist** may recommend lavender on the wound. **Bach flower** remedies' Rescue Remedy diluted in water and applied to the area may help. A **homoeopath** might suggest arnica, taken internally, to help relieve symptoms. Applied gently as an ointment or cream, it will help disperse bruising.

Headaches and migraines

What are they? The most common triggers for headaches include alcohol (hangover) and drugs, allergies, dental problems, eyestrain, head injuries, fever, neck and spine problems including poor posture, depression, anxiety, stress, sinusitis, weather conditions and a poor work environment. Some women experience headaches as a side effect of the contraceptive pill or hormone replacement therapy (HRT). Very occasionally, they may have a more serious cause such as hypertension (sustained rise in blood pressure), brain tumour, temporal arteritis (inflammation of the arteries in the neck, face and scalp) or aneurism (ballooning of a blood vessel) in the brain. Chronic headaches should always be reported to a doctor to establish their cause.

Orthodox treatment The cause of the headache will be addressed first in order to prevent repeated attacks. If self-help remedies such as relaxation or taking mild analgesics do not help, a doctor will give the person a general physical examination and may suggest a visit to the neurologist for further tests.

Reiki treatment To alleviate pain, start by giving Reiki to the part of the head where the pain is most concentrated. If the person feels that the headache might also be caused by tension in the back of the neck and shoulders, treat that area as well. If they feel it has been caused by something they ate, also treat the stomach, liver and pancreas. For most people, concentrating on the general head positions as well as the specific pain area will provide enormous relief, the relaxing effect of Reiki being a major contributor. This treatment can be done at work for a colleague, as they can remain seated at their desk throughout.

Migraines are a chronic complaint and really require several full-body treatments, the number of which will depend on the individual. However, Reiki could be used to give some immediate relief from the symptoms. For this you will need to treat the solar plexus, the temples and the ears.

Other therapies
A **homoeopath** would recommend constitutional treatment for recurrent headaches caused by stress, anxiety or tension. However, a headache which is a symptom of another condition would be treated by specific remedies such as aconite, arnica, bryonia and ruta. An **aromatherapist** might suggest rubbing a little lavender oil into the temples. **Chiropractic** treatment is very helpful in dealing with headaches and migraines of a cervical origin (from the neck). Manipulation of the neck would need to be carried out, as appropriate to the area concerned. A **colour therapist** may suggest that the headaches could be soothed by a restful green colour in the environment, or by visualizations, guided by a tape or whenever possible by a colour therapist.

Shock

What is it? Shock causes a sudden reduction in the supply of blood to the vital organs, such as

Right: Reiki can be extremely effective in eliminating the root cause of headaches brought on by stress and tension. The relaxing effect of a full body treatment can, in itself, help to soothe pain.

the heart, lungs and brain. Mild shock may be brought on by dehydration due to diarrhoea and vomiting, emotional factors and allergic reaction. Symptoms include clammy, pale skin, shallow and rapid breathing, dizziness, anxiety, nausea, restlessness, thirst and vomiting. Severe shock can lead to unconsciousness. This may be caused by heart attack, blood loss or an electric shock.

Orthodox treatment

Treatment for mild shock, for example emotional shock or fainting, is to get the supply of blood to the brain and heart. This can be done by lying the person down and covering them to keep them warm. For emotional shock give comfort and reassurance. For severe shock after an accident

seek emergency medical attention. Other treatment may be required. **Do not** move the patient unless you are sure there are no bone, neck or spinal injuries. If these injuries are absent, raise the legs to get the blood moving to the brain and vital organs. For electric shock, disconnect the power or stand on a dry object and use a wooden broom handle to lever the person away from the electrical source. Give no food or drink to people in severe shock.

Reiki treatment To bring a person out of a state of shock, place your hands in the area of the Third (Solar Plexus) and Fourth (Heart) *Chakras* (see page 23), on the back or front of the body. For a child it is probably more comforting if you put your

arms round them and place your hands on their back.

Other therapies

Bach flower remedies' Rescue Remedy can be applied to the temples and pulse points to reduce symptoms and ease panic. A **homoeopath** may recommend aconite or ignatia, taken every five minutes until the shock has eased. An **aromatherapist** may suggest essential oils of lavender, melissa or peppermint dropped on a handkerchief and held under the nose until help arrives, or the condition stabilizes. **Ayurvedic medicine** offers several treatments for emotional shock, and emergency remedies can be provided while awaiting help. **Western herbalists** can offer calming herbal drinks.

pre- and post-operative reiki

Reiki is very useful in helping people prepare for surgery and recover from it. However, you should not give people Reiki using the distance healing method (see page 38) during surgery as it can alter the level of the anaesthetic and the person may start to wake up. Instead, just before the person goes in for surgery, send Reiki energy using the distance healing method or give it to them directly if you can be at the hospital.

For some people surgery has to be delayed because the surgeon considers that their body is not strong enough to undergo the operation. If this is the case, then give as many full-body treatments as possible to strengthen the person. You can also concentrate on giving Reiki to the area of the body that is to be operated on, after you have treated the whole body. If it is not possible to give the person a hands-on treatment, you can use the distance healing method. I know many people of all ages who have benefited from receiving distance healing treatments for several days before undergoing surgery. Also, many people are extremely apprehensive about surgery and Reiki will help them to deal with their fears and approach their operation in a more relaxed and positive way.

Once the operation is over, Reiki can safely be used to aid a faster recovery. Because you do not need to apply any pressure to the wound or even touch it, you can safely give Reiki without any fear of hurting the recipient. If it is not possible to give a full-body treatment while the person is still in hospital, you can just treat the wound area by holding your hand above it for at least five minutes or longer. You can supplement this treatment by giving a full-body treatment using the distance healing method. Alternatively, you can use the distance method alone. All of these methods can be used on both adults and children.

It takes the body a long time to recover from the trauma of an operation and the effects of anaesthesia. Reiki is such a simple and effective tool in aiding post-operative recovery that if hospitals were to allow Reiki practitioners to treat patients after surgery, they would undoubtedly see some remarkably fast recoveries.

Using the distance healing method also means that you can send Reiki to people in intensive care and to friends and family in hospital overseas. With Reiki, distance does not prevent you from helping and supporting anyone during a time that is traumatic for the individual and also engenders anxiety in the whole family.

reiki for chickenpox

My personal experience of chickenpox confirmed for me the effectiveness of the distance healing method and of Reiki treatment generally.

One Christmas Day my son developed chickenpox. He wasn't very ill and only spent a few hours in bed before he was ready to get up and run around the house. Ever since he had started school I had been dreading him getting chickenpox because I had never had it. I told myself that maybe I wouldn't get it, but that didn't have the desired effect.

Approximately 10 days later I developed what initially felt like flu symptoms but quickly turned into chickenpox. I don't think that I have ever felt as ill as I did in the first couple of days. I immediately started to give myself a full self-treatment several times a day. Although I was still completely incapacitated, the rash was not widespread and, amazingly, it never itched, although I still doused myself in calamine lotion just in case. I had heard such terrible stories from people about how badly chickenpox rash itched, so I was very relieved that I didn't have to go through that. I kept up the daily Reiki treatments as I still had no energy and felt too weak to do anything.

During the time I was ill I was supposed to be organizing a workshop in London for a Reiki Master from Bombay, and although I had already prepared the advertising for it I was unable to do any other preparations. The Reiki Master called to see how things were progressing and I had to tell him that I had been unable to do very much because I had chickenpox. He said he would send me Reiki by the distance method for the next three nights and he hoped that it would help.

On the first night I suddenly started to experience the most excruciating burning pain in my kidneys. They felt as though they were on fire and I could barely stand it. The second and third nights were the same, but when I woke up on the morning of the fourth day, all my symptoms had disappeared. Even though, as a Reiki practitioner, I use the distance healing method all the time for others, I could hardly believe that Reiki energy sent from several thousand miles away could have such a dramatic effect. I spent another few days recovering my strength, but the illness was completely gone. Compared with the experience of other adults, I only had chickenpox for two weeks, which I attribute entirely to the amazing healing power of Reiki.

using reiki with the elderly

Elderly people tend to be isolated in our society. Many are left to live out their later years without their partner and some also have long periods of hospitalization. Even if they do have family and neighbours to talk to, the thing they often miss out on is touch. It is now widely accepted that keeping a pet is extremely beneficial to the health of the elderly – the simple action of stroking a pet replaces the touch of a human. That is why many day hospitals for the elderly now have a communal cat or dog. Many nurses are now training in a technique called Therapeutic Touch, as the health service realizes that nurses can help patients to recover faster through the simple power of touch.

It is also true that the elderly grew up in an era when people were more inhibited about their bodies. For younger generations, the idea of removing your clothes to have a massage does not present much problem, but to the elderly it does. So, although massage would be ideal for the elderly, there are psychological barriers for the majority of them to overcome in order to feel that it is something they would enjoy. Along with the inhibition barrier, the elderly also have a poor body image. This is reinforced by our society's obsession with young, supposedly perfect bodies and our fear of the ageing body, which is seen to represent our ultimate

decay and death and must therefore be hidden away.

Reiki, reflexology, acupuncture and aromatherapy are more appropriate for the elderly, because they are not intrusive in the way massage is. Reiki has a lot to offer, as it is very successful in treating sleeping problems, something that elderly people frequently suffer from, as well as the more chronic conditions such as arthritis. As the Reiki energy goes to the root of the disease it can help to bring the person back into balance, so that they can begin to enjoy a better quality of life. It is never too late for that, and it is also never too late for a person to start the healing process that changes their consciousness, even if they are terminally ill.

As Reiki can be used safely in conjunction with most medication, and will in fact complement its action, it can be very helpful to the elderly. Treating an elderly person with Reiki is no different to treating any other adult, although you may have to take their physical mobility into consideration. For example, if you are treating them at home, can they get onto a treatment table? You may need to consider treating them seated on a dining room chair, with them sitting sideways on it so that you can treat their back. This is not a very relaxing position for them, but it may be the only solution.

If you have Second Degree Reiki (see page 56) you can use the distance healing method. I used this on a lady with a hip problem who would have been unable to get onto a treatment table. I agreed with her a specific time for three days when I would send her Reiki so that she could sit down and focus on the incoming energy.

She told me that every time I sent her Reiki she felt as though she was being wrapped up in a duvet and that she had less pain and more energy after each session.

Reiki is not yet as mainstream as acupuncture or reflexology, but already some healthcare providers are experimenting with bringing in Reiki practitioners to treat their elderly patients. It is to be hoped, it will not be long before they realize the health and economic benefits in terms of a lower drug budget that can be achieved with Reiki.

using reiki with the dying

Dying is a part of living. We may have to face many traumatic events during our life but dying is the one thing that most of us cannot calmly, and certainly not rationally, contemplate. How many stories and myths are based on the quest to live forever, all of them concluding that death cannot be cheated? Certainly there are steps we can take in order to live longer, and there is evidence to suggest that our current average lifespan in the West is nowhere near its maximum potential – but we cannot live forever.

Because receiving Reiki starts a healing process that works holistically on the three levels of the Mind, Body and Spirit, it can help a person to approach the transition of the soul from the body in a way that helps them to understand their life, and, within that, their eventual death. Of course Reiki may reverse the process of a disease that would normally lead to death, but where that happens, the disease will probably be at a less advanced stage and the recipient will be in a different psychological state. It is sometimes better to see Reiki as a means to helping people through their death rather than to see it as a way to keep them alive.

A few years ago, I and another Reiki practitioner were asked if we would give some Reiki treatments to help raise funds for our children's school. We agreed to this, and while we were setting up our treatment table in a quiet corner of the school, I was approached by a lady who told me that she knew about Reiki because her father had received some treatments from a practitioner before he died and that it had completely changed him. When I embarked upon the writing of this book I contacted her, because what she said then had stayed in my mind, and she very kindly took the time to tell me the full story.

Sarah's father was a man who was from a conservative Calvinistic background, and who had often been distant from his daughter. He was diagnosed with bowel cancer in 1987 and, following an operation, was told he had a 95 per cent chance of survival. Not long after this it was discovered that the cancer had spread to his

liver and that he needed another operation. He refused the operation and decided to go it alone. He moved back to his birthplace, which coincidentally had a growing New Age community. There he decided to try alternative medicine, a choice that was uncharacteristic for him. He chose to have Reiki treatments and told Sarah about how he experienced feeling great heat in certain areas of his body that afterwards allayed the symptoms of the disease. The treatments did not cure him and within seven months he died. However, receiving Reiki opened his mind and allowed him to make peace with his life, with his daughter and with his faith in God.

We often confuse healing with curing a disease, which is a short-term way of looking at it. In this story the healing in the death process was spiritual and emotional, embracing both father and daughter, and the effects are much more long term than any physical cure.

giving birth with reiki

At the other end of the spectrum from death lies birth. Though we barely stop to consider it, a birth is a momentous event. We bring a new life onto the Earth, a life with a unique soul and spirit and a physical body and characteristics that are inherited from both parents and from their families, going back many generations. As parents we are responsible for nurturing this new life and giving the child every chance to reach their full potential. So we take care to feed the child properly, to educate them mentally and spiritually and to protect them from all harm. We can also take care of our children before they are born and during their birth, by caring for our own bodies and by ensuring that the birth process is as free from trauma as possible. Reiki can assist in both of these.

During pregnancy, both mother and baby can benefit from regular Reiki treatments. Some of the symptoms of pregnancy that mothers find it hard to cope with, such as sickness, excessive tiredness and backache, can be alleviated by Reiki. It can also support the mother through this time of emotional upheaval, particularly if it is a first baby, and help her come to understand the meaning of motherhood. Additionally, it can help her to bond with the baby before birth. Many mothers I know, myself included, get to a stage during

pregnancy when they feel that their body is being taken over by this 'thing' and that they no longer own their bodies. I feel that Reiki can help mothers to work through this feeling of negativity towards their baby and instead have a positive understanding of their role in producing life. Giving a Reiki treatment is also a way for fathers to become more intimately involved in antenatal care and to form a pre-birth bond with the baby in a very different way. Most people I have spoken to find that giving Reiki to a pregnant woman is an awesome experience, as both the practitioner and the mother can feel the baby trying to move towards the energy during the treatment. Therefore, if both parents are Reiki practitioners they are able to share this experience and the mother can give self-treatments daily.

This will prepare both baby and parents for the birth. However, even if a mother is not able to have Reiki treatments throughout her pregnancy, mother and baby can still benefit from receiving Reiki during the birth. The perfect situation would be to have a Reiki practitioner with you when you are giving birth – ideally the father. If this is not possible, the distance healing method will be just as successful. If you know several Reiki practitioners, ask them if they will take it in turns to send you Reiki once you have started labour. Arrange for each one to phone the next and so on. As labour can be very long and a distance healing session takes only about 15 minutes, you can also agree with them in advance the number of times they send Reiki. Involving several people in sending Reiki will increase the intensity of

the energy, but it also works with just one person sending the Reiki, as in the following case study.

My friend Anne was expecting her first baby. At various times during the early stages of her pregnancy I mentioned that Reiki treatments would be very beneficial to her and the baby. However, both of us were busy with work and as we live some distance from each other, we never managed to find the time.

Before we knew it, there were only a few weeks left before the baby was due. Up until then Anne's pregnancy had progressed very easily, with only a few minor complaints. However, a routine scan seemingly showed that the baby was underweight for the due

date and Anne was ordered to rest in bed for a week. Naturally, she was extremely distressed about this, and although she had been anticipating having a normal delivery, her gynaecologist warned her that a Caesarean might be necessary for the sake of the baby.

It was at this point I realized that the best thing I could do was to send her Reiki using the distance healing method. I did this several times during the week that she was resting. Her next scan revealed that the baby had put on some weight that week, and although there was now less concern about that, Anne and her husband decided to proceed with an elective Caesarean.

I sent Anne Reiki the night before she went into hospital and then again about 30 minutes before she went into the operating room. A short time later, Anne's husband called to let me know that they had a lovely son who turned out not to be underweight at all.

I visited Anne the next evening, and as might be expected she was in pain from the incision but was otherwise feeling and looking extremely well. I gave her Reiki over the site of the Caesarean incision without touching it, for about 5–10 minutes. The next day I sent Reiki to Anne, clearly visualizing all of her but focusing on the lower abdomen. I did this for several more days. When she came home from hospital, the health visitors who attended her were amazed to find that her scar was almost healed. So was Anne, as typically she does not heal fast and often gets infections when wounds are healing. She also recovered from the Caesarean much faster than anyone else I have known who has had one.

It is sometimes thought that complementary therapies are only appropriate for those who believe in 'natural childbirth'. I think that this story shows that Reiki can successfully be used in combination with orthodox medicine and that the recipient can believe in and benefit from both at the same time without feeling that they are compromising either approach.

Below: Both mother and baby can benefit greatly from Reiki treatment during all stages of pregnancy. Reiki can be helpful for easing symptoms such as morning sickness and fatigue which often occur in the early stages.

Glossary

Acupuncture
The Chinese believe that energy, *Chi*, runs through our bodies along pathways called meridians. Acupuncture uses needles to stimulate points along the meridians, to promote the flow of *Chi*. It is good for pain control.

Aromatherapy
This uses the essential oils from aromatic plants to promote vitality of the body, and serenity of mind. It alleviates stress, improves mood, and is a treatment for many minor disorders.

Auricular therapy
A form of acupuncture focusing on the ear. It is good for pain control, and can help with changing unwanted patterns of behaviour.

Ayurveda
The Indian science of life. Ayurveda assesses the individual and all their circumstances, giving advice on nutrition, exercise and lifestyle, as well as offering medication.

Bach flower remedies
These provide support for any condition involving emotional issues – despondency, anxiety, etc., and help counteract the effects of stress.

Chiropractic
Treatment for the musculo-skeletal system, and supporting nerves, with particular emphasis on the spine. Practitioners offer a range of manipulative techniques, aiming to increase mobility in joints, and overcome problems originating in the soft tissues.

Colour therapy
The use of colour to treat mental, emotional and physical problems and restore the whole person to health and harmony. It is sometimes used with other therapies and can help relieve insomnia, depression and stress-related problems.

Homoeopathy
A homoeopathic remedy is one which produces the same symptoms as those the sick person experiences, and in doing so provokes the body into throwing them off. Like may be cured by like is the basic principle of homeopathic therapeutics.

Nutritional therapy
Diet is used to prevent illness and treat specific conditions, such as migraine. Issues addressed include food allergies, nutritional deficiencies and toxic overload.

Reflexology
Pressure is applied to points on the feet, and sometimes the hands. By a reflex action this stimulates energy flow to a related muscle or organ, and thus promotes healing.

Tai Chi / Qigong
These gentle, Chinese practices use flowing exercises to help improve the flow of *Chi* (energy) through the body, and thus maintain or improve physical and mental health.

Western herbalism
This uses plant remedies in the treatment of disease. Plant remedies are extracts from a part of the whole plant (e.g. roots, berries) and contain hundreds of constituents. Active constituents are balanced by the numerous other substances present.

Yoga
Originally an Indian therapy, yoga is an effective way of promoting flexibility and strength in mind and body. It can improve posture, muscle tone, and mobility, and bring a sense of peace in a stressful world.

bibliography

General books

Bamforth, Nick. *Trusting the Healer Within*. Amethyst Books, London, 1989

Chia, Mantak and Maneewan. *Awaken Healing Light of the Tao*. Huntington, N Y, Healing Tao Books, 1993

Fontana, David. *The Secret Language of Symbols*. Piatkus, London, 1997

Gawain, Shakti. *Creative Visualization*. Bantam, London, 1982

Krystal, Phyllis. *Cutting the Ties That Bind* and *Cutting More Ties That Bind*. Samuel Weiser, York Beach, Maine, USA, 1993

MacRitchie, James. *Chi Kung – Cultivating Personal Energy*. Element Books, Shaftesbury, Dorset, 1993

Ozaniec, Naomi. *Chakras for Beginners*. Headway/Hodder & Stoughton, London, 1994

Price, Shirley. *Practical Aromatherapy*. Thorsons, London, 1994

White, Ruth. *Working with your Chakras*. Piatkus, London, 1993

Reiki books

Baginski, Bodo & Sharamon, Shalila. *Reiki: Universal Life Energy*. Life Rhythm Publications, California, USA, 1988

Haberly, Helen J. *Reiki: Hawayo Takata's Story*. Archedigm Publications, 1990

Horan, Paula. *Empowerment through Reiki*. Lotus Light, Silver Lake, Wisconsin, USA, 1990

Lübeck, Walter. *Reiki for First Aid*. Lotus Light, Silver Lake, Wisconsin, USA, 1995

Petter, Frank A. *Reiki Fire*. Lotus Light, Silver Lake, Wisconsin, USA, 1997

Stein, Diane. *Essential Reiki*. The Crossing Press, Watsonville, California, USA, 1995

index

acknowledgements

The publishers would like to thank the following organizations for the loan of props and accessories:

Virgo Bodywork Tables, PO Box 13835, London, N15

Tavy Covers, 'Kimberleigh', Bolt House Close, Tavistock, Devon PL16 8LN

Aura-Soma, South Road, Tetford, Horncastle, Lincolnshire LN9 6QB

Useful addresses

The Reiki Association, Tel: 01981 550829

Don Alexander, Reiki, BCM Avatar, London, WC1N 3XX

The publishers would like to thank the following individuals and organizations for their kind permission to reproduce photographs in this book:

AKG, London 65, /Galleria dell' Accademia, Venice 64.

Bridgeman Art Library/Cott Nero DIV f.94v St. Mark, cross carpet page Lindisfarne Gospels (c.698 AD) British Library, London/Bridgeman Art Library, London/New York 63.

Reed Consumer Books Ltd./Peter Myers Front Cover, front flap, back cover, back flap, 1, 2-3, 4-5, 8-9, 11, 12, 13-14, 17, 19, 23, 25 left, 25 right, 26 top right, 26-27 centre, 27, 28, 29, 30 top left, 31 bottom right, 32 bottom left, 32-33, 34, 34-35 centre, 36-37 centre, 37, 38, 39, 40-41 bottom centre right, 42-43, 45, 47, 50-51, 55, 57, 59, 60, 61, 66-67, 69, 70-71 top centre, 71 bottom centre, 71 bottom left, 71 centre right, 72 bottom left, 72 top left, 72 top right, 72-73 bottom centre, 73 top centre, 73 centre, 74 top, 74-75 bottom centre, 75 top, 75 bottom centre right, 76 top, 77 bottom right, 77 top, 78 bottom, 78-79 top centre, 79 bottom right, 80-81, 83, 84-85 top centre, 85 bottom left, 85 top right, 86 top, 86 bottom, 87 centre left, 87 bottom left, 87 bottom right, 87 top left, 88 top, 88 bottom, 89 top, 89 bottom, 90 bottom left, 90 centre right, 90 top, 91 top, 91 bottom, 92 bottom right, 92 top left, 93, 94 centre right, 94 bottom left, 94 top left, 95, 96 top, 96 bottom, 97 top, 97 bottom, 98, 99, 100-101, 102 centre left, 102-103 bottom centre, 103 top left, 104-105, 107, 109, 110-111, 113, 115, 116-117 top centre, 118-119 bottom centre, 120-121 bottom centre right, 123, 124, 125.

Phyllis Lei Furumoto 46, 48, 49 left, 49 top centre.

Publishing Director: Laura Bamford
Executive Editor: Jane McIntosh
Editors: Catharine Davey
Arlene Sobel
Diana Vowles
Creative Director: Keith Martin
Senior Designer: Geoff Fennell
Photography: Peter Myers
Stylist: Leeann Mackenzie
Picture Research: Zoe Holtermann
Production Controller: Julie Hadingham

First published in Great Britain in 1998 by Hamlyn, an imprint of Octopus Publishing Group Ltd, 81 Fulham Road, London SW3 6RB

Copyright © Octopus Publishing Group Ltd
Reprinted in 1998
ISBN 0 600 59528 5

A CIP catalogue of this book is available on request.

Printed in Hong Kong